FRESHWATER
BIRDS

© AA Media Limited 2011

Written by Andrew Cleave

Produced for AA Publishing by D & N Publishing, Baydon, Wiltshire

Commissioning editor at AA Publishing: Paul Mitchell
Production at AA Publishing: Rachel Davis

Printed and bound in China by C&C Offset Printing Co. Ltd

A CIP catalogue record for this book is available from the British Library.

ISBN 978-0-7495-6926-6
        978-0-7495-6936-5 (SS)

The contents of this publication are believed correct at the time of printing. Nevertheless, the publishers cannot be held responsible for any errors or omissions or for changes in the details given in this guide or for the consequences of any reliance on the information provided by the same. This does not affect your statutory rights.

Published by AA Publishing, a trading name of AA Media Limited, whose registered office is Fanum House, Basing View, Basingstoke, Hampshire RG21 4EA. Registered number 06112600.

A04089
theAA.com/shop

CONTENTS

Birds are the most popular and conspicuous components of our wildlife, and we all come across them in everyday life. They tend to be lively and vocal, many are large and colourful and, as a group, they are not so numerous that it is difficult to get to know the commoner species. In addition, their mastery of the air remains a source of wonder to humans.

The *AA Spotter Guide to Freshwater Birds* covers the species of bird most likely to be seen in England, Scotland and Wales during our day-to-day urban and rural lives, and others that may be found in some of the remoter parts of Britain. Most are common and widespread, and include some of our most familiar birds. Some species with a very restricted range are included, while others may have particular habitat requirements and be harder to find. Some attractive and distinctive or large and powerful species are also included to provide inspiration for excursions to some of the more remote parts of Britain.

Each species is given two full pages, and the text is concise so that as much information as possible can be packed into the available space. Each species account begins with the common English name and is followed by the species' scientific name. The subsequent text is divided into sections: **FACT FILE**, which covers the species' size, habitat preferences, food and voice; **IDENTIFICATION**, which describes its appearance; **STATUS AND HABITS**, which describes where the species occurs (if a specific range is not given, the species is widespread across Britain in suitable habitats), its population status, and behavioural traits that assist with identification; and **KEY FACT**, which provides tips on unique information separating this species from close relatives. The photographs are of adults unless indicated otherwise.

The POCHARD is a familiar diving duck on large bodies of fresh water. It is commonest in the winter months.

BIRDS ARE A group of vertebrates that are distinguished by having feathers, and that are generally able to fly. The ability to fly enables birds to exploit many habitats and sources of food, flee harsh weather, escape from predators, or display to other birds in the breeding season. The size and colour of different feather groups (called tracts) on a bird enable us to identify different species; examples of this are shown on the topography diagram below.

After mating, female birds lay eggs in a nest, which can be an open construction of varied size and complexity, or a hole in a tree or building. The eggs are then incubated by either or both parents until the chicks hatch. Chicks of small birds and birds of prey tend to be fairly helpless and nestbound, entirely dependent on their parents for the first few days of life, whereas waterfowl chicks often leave the nest and are able to follow their parents within a day of hatching. They are taught by their parents how to find food.

Many birds are migratory, some travelling huge distances across the globe. Species that spend the northern temperate summer in Britain arrive from the warmer tropics to the south, returning there before the onset of our winter. Our winter bird populations, meanwhile, are enhanced by the arrival of other species from further north and east.

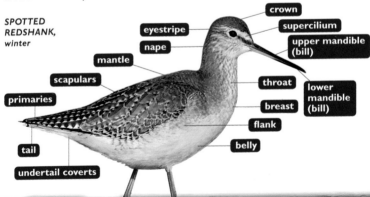

SPOTTED REDSHANK, winter

crown
supercilium
upper mandible (bill)
eyestripe
nape
mantle
scapulars
throat
lower mandible (bill)
breast
primaries
flank
belly
tail
undertail coverts

FINDING AND STUDYING FRESHWATER BIRDS

MANY FRESHWATER BIRDS are easy to find, as they live their lives alongside people, be it in parks in our towns and cities, or in the wider countryside where rivers, lakes, ponds and man-made habitats such as gravel pits and reservoirs provide feeding and breeding sites for them. Ducks, geese and swans are frequently seen in city centre parks, and what may be thought of as coastal birds – including several gull species – are nowadays regular urban visitors. A lunchtime break in a city park could provide the opportunity to get close views of some of our commonest birds as well as the most colourful. Anglers, meanwhile, will be very familiar with some of the freshwater species that share the riverside with them, while a visit to a large lake or reservoir will give the opportunity to see different waterbirds such as diving ducks, grebes and martins.

Springtime sees the arrival from the south of migrant warblers, swallows, martins and terns, summer is a busy season for nesting and rearing young, while the autumn brings visitors from the north, fleeing the onset of harsh conditions in the Arctic. Swans, ducks and waders find the relatively mild conditions in Britain, and its ice-free open waters, the ideal location for the winter. So whatever the season, freshwater habitats will attract a good selection of birds.

Freshwater habitats range from tumbling mountain streams, home to Dippers and Grey Wagtails, to large, open expanses of deep water where diving ducks and grebes are more common. Reedbeds build up on shallow margins, and these provide perfect cover for smaller birds such as warblers and the Bearded Tit, while secretive species like the Water Rail or Bittern may live, unseen but often heard, in the depths of the reeds. Marshes and flood-meadows, with ditches and streams running across them, are ideal for many species of wader, and in winter they are often home to huge flocks of wildfowl. Man-made habitats are also of great importance – ornamental lakes, gravel pits, canals, Watercress beds and garden ponds can all support different bird species. Freshwater birds show a huge range of adaptations to their environment, with a great variety of bill shapes, leg lengths, feeding habits and migration patterns, all designed to cope with the varied niches they inhabit.

It is easy to make your birdwatching purposeful, and for your sightings to help the conservation of birds and other wildlife. The British Trust for Ornithology (www.bto.org.uk) organises a range of surveys that rely on volunteers submitting records of the birds they have seen. You can take part in a survey of the birds that visit your garden, breeding birds of the wider countryside, and winter waterfowl of our coasts, estuaries and lakes. The trust also has an online facility, called BirdTrack, that allows you to keep and access your observation records while contributing data on a local, national and international level. Conservation also relies on observers taking care not to interfere with breeding birds, and allowing flocks of winter visitors to get on with the business of feeding, preening and loafing without disturbance.

GLOSSARY

Cryptic Camouflaged.
Eclipse Moulted plumage of ducks in summer, which for a short period renders them flightless; eclipse males resemble females.
Hybridisation Interbreeding of two different species.
Incubation Sitting on eggs to keep them warm in the period up to hatching.
Invertebrates All animals that lack a backbone, including insects.
Juvenile Young bird in its first year, but not yet in full adult plumage.
Lek Communal display ground.
Migration Mass regular movement of bird populations from one geographical region to another.
Preening Care of feathers, usually by passing feather edges through the bill.
Primaries Strong, long flight feathers occupying the outer third and tip of the wing.
Speculum Colourful band near the rear edge of a duck's wing.
Supercilium Eyebrow, often forming a clear, pale stripe on the side of the head.
Tertials Flight feathers occupying the inner third of the wing.
Watermeadow Area of grassland that is periodically flooded, usually in the winter.

MUTE SWAN
Cygnus olor

FACT FILE

SIZE Length 145–160cm **HABITAT** Large, slow rivers and canals, lakes, sheltered coasts, freshwater marshes **FOOD** Plant material; occasional small invertebrates, often collected by stretching neck down into deep water **VOICE** Usually silent

IDENTIFICATION

Adults have all-white plumage, although neck and head may be stained by muddy water. Large bill is orange-red with a large black knob at base, largest in male. Juveniles have buff-brown plumage and a dull pink bill, but moult into adult plumage in first winter. Neck is held in a graceful S-shape when swimming. Wings make whistling sounds in flight.

KEY FACT Male swans can be quite aggressive in the nesting season, fearlessly chasing off intruders with a great deal of hissing and wing-flapping. This 'busking' behaviour can be directed at humans as well as other swans.

MALE

LOCATION	DATE/TIME

STATUS AND HABITS

The commonest swan and likely to be seen in a range of watery habitats, from city parks to lakes, rivers and coasts. Large weedy nests are built close to water, with both birds in attendance. Swans often feed by upending in deep water, using their long necks to reach food that is out of range of other waterbirds. Large 'herds' of swans may gather in good feeding areas after the breeding season, and many move to the coast in winter.

FEMALE

WHOOPER SWAN
Cygnus cygnus

SIZE Length 145–160cm HABITAT Winter visitor to
flood-meadows, stubble fields, lochs FOOD Aquatic vegetation,
spilt grain VOICE Loud bugling calls, usually given in flight

FACT FILE

IDENTIFICATION

Large, long-necked swan. Adults are pure white, although head and neck
may sometimes be stained orange with mud; feet and legs are black. Large
bill is black towards tip and bright yellow at base. Juveniles have pinkish-
buff plumage and a dark pink bill that becomes paler towards base.

LOCATION	DATE/TIME

STATUS AND HABITS

A winter visitor to Britain from breeding grounds on Arctic tundra and lake shores. Flocks appear in the autumn, choosing regular overwintering sites where they can find food and safety. They often fly in V-formation, calling loudly to each other. When feeding they graze on open marshes, constantly on the lookout for danger and usually keeping to open areas well away from human disturbance. They are unlikely to mix with the smaller Bewick's Swan.

KEY FACT

Family groups migrate S together in the autumn and remain with each other through most of the winter, the juveniles recognisable by their greyish plumage.

BEWICK'S SWAN
Cygnus columbianus

FACT FILE

SIZE Length 115–125cm **HABITAT** Winter visitor to flood-meadows, coastal marshes, shallow lake margins
FOOD Aquatic vegetation, roots and shoots, spilt grain
VOICE Various far-carrying bugling calls, usually given in flight

IDENTIFICATION

Smallest European swan. Adults have all-white plumage, black legs and feet, and a black bill with a small, variable yellow area at base; individual birds can be recognised by the shape of this area. Juveniles have buff-grey plumage and a dull pink bill with a darker tip, and can be distinguished from juvenile **Whooper Swans** by association with the adults.

LOCATION	DATE/TIME

KEY FACT

Individual birds can be recognised by their unique bill markings, each having a distinctive black and yellow pattern at the base of the bill. This has enabled researchers to recognise the same birds year after year at the same sites and confirm mated pairs remain together.

STATUS AND HABITS

A winter visitor to Britain from remote breeding grounds on Siberian tundra. Birds regularly return to the same overwintering sites, migrating in flocks and with family groups remaining together. In very harsh weather, birds move further **W** to escape freezing conditions.

GREYLAG GOOSE
Anser anser

SIZE Length 75–90cm **HABITAT** Farmland, grassland, marshes, lakes **FOOD** Grass, clovers, spilt grain **VOICE** Various nasal, cackling calls, similar to those of domestic geese

IDENTIFICATION
A large, stocky goose with mostly grey-brown plumage, pink legs and an orange bill, but look out for migrant birds from the **E**, which have pink bills. In flight, wings show contrasting light grey forewings and dark trailing edges, and some birds have a few dark bars on underside. Tail is mostly white with a dark band.

LOCATION	DATE/TIME

STATUS AND HABITS

A common and familiar bird of lowland areas, sometimes associating with Canada Geese. Usually found in small family groups feeding on open grassland, but always on the alert for danger and ready to fly off noisily if disturbed. They gather in larger flocks in the autumn and winter, when new arrivals may migrate to  Britain. Genuine wild birds may be hard to identify as there have been many escapes and introductions, making this a very widespread species.

KEY FACT

In Britain, Greylag Geese tend not to migrate, so this is the only grey goose likely to be encountered in large numbers during the summer. When nesting they are quite secretive, but once the goslings have hatched family parties become a frequent sight on lakes and marshes.

PINK-FOOTED GOOSE
Anser brachyrhynchus

FACT FILE

SIZE Length 60–75cm **HABITAT** Winter visitor to fields, marshes, lake margins **FOOD** Plant material, especially grasses and clovers **VOICE** Musical two- or three-note honking calls

IDENTIFICATION

A small, compact grey goose. Adults have pink legs and feet, and a dark bill with a variable pink patch that sometimes forms a band across the middle. Head and neck are dark brown, contrasting with paler underside and greyish back. Wings look pale in flight, but show darker flight feathers. Juveniles are similar but with dull pink legs.

LOCATION	DATE/TIME

KEY FACT Harsh conditions in the species' Arctic nesting sites mean that in some years no young are raised, but these are long-lived birds and their numbers can build up in good years. They are still persecuted by hunters in some areas, but many of their traditional wintering grounds are now protected.

STATUS AND HABITS

Huge flocks of Pink-footed Geese migrate to Britain in the autumn from their Arctic breeding grounds, forming a thrilling spectacle as they fly in to their traditional coastal roost sites as night falls. During the day they spread out to feed on marshes and grasslands, but at dusk they fly to the safety of coastal marshes, with noisy skeins of geese converging into vast flocks, and 'wiffling', or tilting to the side, as they descend to the ground, finally falling silent in the dark.

BEAN GOOSE
Anser fabalis

FACT FILE

SIZE Length 65–80cm **HABITAT** Scarce winter visitor to farmland, stubble fields and marshes
FOOD Plant material, roots, shoots, grain
VOICE Harsh, cackling calls; deep, two- or three-note honks

IDENTIFICATION

A medium-sized goose with mostly chocolate-brown coloration, orange legs and feet, and a relatively long neck. Bill is dark, but with varying amounts of orange, depending on race. In flight, wings look mostly dark.

fabalis

LOCATION	DATE/TIME

KEY FACT Birds with extensive orange on their bill are *fabalis* subspecies from boreal forest regions, while birds with a small orange bill patch are members of the *rossicus* subspecies from Siberian tundra.

rossicus

STATUS AND HABITS

A scarce winter visitor to Britain from N Scandinavia and Arctic Russia, occurring mainly in the E and preferring open farmland and wetlands. Small family groups may sometimes be spotted among other grey geese. Shy and nervous, Bean Geese can be difficult to observe closely, and prefer to be in very open habitats.

WHITE-FRONTED GOOSE
Anser albifrons

FACT FILE

SIZE **Length 65–85cm** HABITAT **Watermeadows, estuaries, marshes, grasslands** FOOD **Grasses, roots, buds and shoots, spilt grain** VOICE **Musical, ringing flock calls; hissing, cackling calls on ground**

IDENTIFICATION

A large grey goose. Adults have a distinctive white forehead, and pinkish-orange legs and feet. Plumage is grey-brown above and paler below, with variable dark bands across belly. Wings look dark in flight and tail shows white below with a dark terminal band. Juveniles resemble adults but lack white forehead.

KEY FACT Birds of the Siberian *albifrons* subspecies have a pinkish bill, while birds of the Greenland *flavirostris* subspecies have an orange-yellow bill.

LOCATION	DATE/TIME

STATUS AND HABITS

A nervous and wary goose, difficult to watch at close quarters but often seen in huge flocks flying in 'V' formation, calling loudly. Up to 30,000 members of the Greenland race overwinter in Ireland, Scotland and Wales, with smaller numbers of the Siberian race overwintering in S England.

BARNACLE GOOSE
Branta leucopsis

FACT FILE

SIZE Length 60–75cm **HABITAT** Coastal grasslands, marshes, grazing land **FOOD** Roots, grasses, seeds **VOICE** Short, staccato barking calls

IDENTIFICATION

A small, compact goose, looking mostly black and white from a distance and in flight. Adults have a white face and black neck, with a black bill and eye. Back is barred black and grey, and underside is white with grey barring on flanks. Legs and feet are black. Juveniles have a more blotchy appearance.

LOCATION	DATE/TIME

STATUS AND HABITS

A winter visitor from the Arctic to marshes and grasslands, mainly in **NW** Scotland, but smaller numbers occur further **S**. Large flocks descend on

grasslands, often settling on agricultural land where grazing is better. At dawn they fly in noisy flocks to feed on grasslands, leaving at dusk for safe roosting sites. Family groups stay together, and whole breeding populations migrate together to the same overwintering areas.

KEY FACT

Barnacle Geese have no connection with the Goose Barnacle, a marine organism, their names having arisen centuries ago through confusion over their origins. They do not feed on barnacles, being entirely vegetarian.

CANADA GOOSE
Branta canadensis

FACT FILE

SIZE Length 90–100cm **HABITAT** Lakes, gravel pits, city parks, grasslands near rivers **FOOD** Aquatic vegetation, grasses, roots, shoots, seeds **VOICE** Loud, two-note honking calls; trumpeting sounds

IDENTIFICATION

Britain's largest goose, with mostly brown plumage. Head and neck are black with a large white patch on face. Legs and feet are black. In flight, undertail area looks white and flight feathers are black. Goslings are yellowish brown.

KEY FACT Very occasionally a genuine migrant Canada Goose turns up; these birds are often of a much smaller subspecies and are usually very nervous, keeping away from the resident birds.

LOCATION	DATE/TIME

STATUS AND HABITS

Introduced to Britain in the 17th century, the Canada Goose is now well established here, often thriving in urban parks, where they are less wary of humans than other geese. Present year-round, flocks gather in favourable feeding areas in winter, family groups remaining close together. In the nesting season they are more secretive and find their

own safe spot, taking the goslings to the water soon after they hatch. Flocks fly in noisy V-formation, returning to safe roosting sites at dusk.

EGYPTIAN GOOSE
Alopochen aegyptiacus

FACT FILE

SIZE Length 65–73cm **HABITAT** Fields and marshes close to lakes and rivers **FOOD** Leaves, shoots, seeds **VOICE** Loud, braying calls

IDENTIFICATION

A small goose with mostly brown plumage. Head, neck and underside of adults are pale buff-brown but show a contrasting dark collar, eye-patch and chest patch. In flight, wings show large white patches, and there is a glossy green speculum. Bill and long legs are pink. Juveniles are similar but lack dark eye-patch and chest patch.

LOCATION	DATE/TIME

STATUS AND HABITS

Aggressive and quarrelsome,
Egyptian Geese are usually found
in small, isolated populations, not
readily mixing with each other
or with other species. They prefer
lush vegetation and sometimes
remain hidden in long
grass, but may also be seen
perching in trees. River banks
and lake margins where they
can nest in deep cover, but
easily reach good feeding
areas, are their preferred
habitats, and they have
managed to spread over a
wide area by dispersing along
rivers and canals.

KEY FACT

An introduced
species in Britain, which has
become well established in parts
of S and E England, despite its
African origins.

ADULTS FIGHTING

SHELDUCK
Tadorna tadorna

FACT FILE

SIZE Length 60–70cm HABITAT Coastal marshes, muddy shores, inland gravel pits and lakes
FOOD Small molluscs and crustaceans
VOICE Male whistles; female quacks

IDENTIFICATION
Bright red bill and pinkish legs of adults contrast with glossy, dark green head and neck and pale plumage, and with dark orange chest band and dark bands along wings. Sexes are alike, but males are larger and have a large knob at base of bill. Juveniles are more mottled, with a dull pink bill.

MALE

LOCATION	DATE/TIME

STATUS AND HABITS

Although most Shelducks live along coasts, the species has spread inland where there are gravel pits, large lakes and rivers with muddy margins. They feed by sweeping the bill from side to side over mud to sieve out tiny molluscs or shrimps; the margins of the bill have comb-like edges that act as filters. After the breeding season, large numbers of Shelducks gather at traditional sites on marshes to moult their flight feathers, before dispersing again in winter.

MALES

KEY FACT

Nests are built in deep cover, under dense bushes and even in old Rabbit holes. Females defend their young aggressively, and take them to the water soon after they hatch.

RUDDY SHELDUCK
Tadorna ferruginea

SIZE Length 61–67cm **HABITAT** Wetlands, especially large rivers **FOOD** Plant material, small invertebrates **VOICE** Nasal, honking *ang* sounds

FACT FILE

IDENTIFICATION

A distinctive large duck with rusty orange-brown plumage, a lighter head and neck, and contrasting dark eyes, bill, legs and feet. At rest, wings have black wingtips but in flight they show a striking black and white pattern. Sexes are similar but female has a paler head. Juveniles have dull versions of adult plumage.

KEY FACT

A very attractive and eye-catching species, popular in wildfowl collections, but sometimes able to escape and establish small feral populations.

MALE

LOCATION	DATE/TIME

STATUS AND HABITS

A rare visitor to Britain, with some genuine migrants and some escapes from captivity. A hole-nesting species, sometimes choosing tree-holes or derelict waterside buildings. Young enter water soon after hatching and are tended by both parents, although they can feed for themselves. Rarely found far from water, although they will migrate long distances.

FEMALE

MALLARD
Anas platyrhynchos

FACT FILE

SIZE Length 50–65cm **HABITAT** Wide range of wetland habitats, including urban sites **FOOD** Wide range of plant and animal foods, scraps **VOICE** Males have weak nasal calls; females quack

IDENTIFICATION

Males have mostly grey-brown plumage, but head is glossy green with a yellow bill, and breast is chestnut below white collar. When dabbling, black stern and white tail show clearly. Moulting males in summer are similar to females, which are mostly mottled brown with a darker bill. In flight, both sexes show a white-edged blue speculum. Juveniles resemble female.

KEY FACT This is one of our most abundant wildfowl species, with up to 350,000 pairs breeding in Britain each year, and many more arriving in the winter from colder N regions.

MALE

LOCATION	DATE/TIME

STATUS AND HABITS

A common, widespread and familiar bird, found in habitats ranging from city parks to lakes, rivers and coasts. Often very confident around people, readily taking food scraps and becoming very tame, but when nesting the females are extremely secretive, concealing their nests in deep vegetation, often away from the water. Large numbers occur on lakes and rivers, usually associating with other wildfowl, but isolated pairs can also be found on remote ponds and streams. Freezing weather drives them to the coast.

FEMALE

GADWALL
Anas strepera

SIZE Length 45–55cm **HABITAT** Large lakes, gravel pits, marshes **FOOD** Seeds, plant roots and shoots, invertebrates **VOICE** Males have short nasal calls; females quack

IDENTIFICATION
Male is the least strikingly marked of the ducks, with mostly grey-brown plumage, which at close range shows delicate vermiculations on flanks. Bill is dark, and tail and stern are all dark. Female resembles a slim female Mallard, with a yellowish bill and brown plumage. In flight, both sexes show a white speculum and very pale underwing. Juveniles are similar to female.

KEY FACT The female Gadwall is very tricky to identify, except when associating with the male, but even in mixed flocks pairs will often remain close together, allowing easy identification.

MALE

LOCATION	DATE/TIME

STATUS AND HABITS

Gadwalls are quite widespread, but never found in large numbers anywhere in their range apart from in winter, when they gather on lakes and marshes, sometimes associating with large flocks of Coots. In the breeding season they are very secretive, and only the presence of lone males on a lake gives a clue to females nesting nearby. A few thousand pairs breed in Britain, with more joining them from the N in harsh winters.

FEMALE

WIGEON
Anas penelope

FACT FILE

SIZE Length 45–51cm HABITAT Breeds on lakes; winters on coastal grasslands and estuaries FOOD Plant leaves and shoots, especially eelgrasses and algae VOICE Males have shrill *whee-ooo* calls; females make quiet churring sounds

IDENTIFICATION

An attractive dabbling duck with a colourful appearance in good light. Male has an orange head with a yellow crown, and a pink-tinged breast. Most of the plumage is grey above, but underside is white and stern black. Female is mostly brown with a white belly and dull orange flanks. In flight, female's wings look dark, but male's show large white patches. Juveniles resemble female.

KEY FACT

The wintering population of Wigeon in Britain greatly exceeds the summer breeding population, as many thousands of birds from Iceland and N Scandinavia head for our ice-free estuaries and coastal marshes.

MALE

LOCATION	DATE/TIME

STATUS AND HABITS

In the breeding season **Wigeons** are very shy, and are confined mainly to remote N areas such as upland lakes and peat bogs, where they live fairly solitary lives. In winter, however, they all head for the coast, especially large estuaries where they can feed on algae as the tide retreats. At high tide they move to nearby coastal grasslands and marshes in conspicuous and noisy flocks that sometimes take off together, calling loudly.

FEMALE

TEAL
Anas crecca

SIZE Length 34–38cm HABITAT Shallow lakes and ponds in summer; flood-meadows and coastal marshes in winter FOOD Invertebrates, seeds VOICE Chirping, high-pitched *krick*

FACT FILE

IDENTIFICATION

Smallest duck of the region, with a compact shape and distinctive plumage. Males have an orange-brown head with a large yellow-edged green patch over eye running back to nape. Back and flanks are mostly grey and underparts are white. Rear view shows a black stern with creamy-yellow side patches. Females and juveniles are similar, with grey-brown plumage. All show a green speculum and white underwing in flight.

KEY FACT Most Teals that breed in N Europe head SW in winter, mainly to Britain's coasts, although some travel even further – as far as North Africa. All migrate N again in spring.

MALE

LOCATION	DATE/TIME

STATUS AND HABITS

A widespread and, in some places, very common duck, present year-round in Britain, but very secretive in the breeding season. When alarmed, Teals take off vertically with rapid wingbeats and a swerving flight, soon dropping into cover again. Flocks often fly in formation, resembling waders. They prefer to feed in shallow water, sifting soft mud with side-to-side bill movements. Huge flocks congregate in winter after leaving N breeding grounds, but hunting pressure makes them very wary of humans.

FEMALE

GARGANEY
Anas querquedula

SIZE Length 37–41cm HABITAT Marshes, flood-meadows, lake margins FOOD Aquatic plants and invertebrates VOICE Male makes a distinctive wooden-sounding rattle; female gives quiet quacks

IDENTIFICATION

Male is easily recognised, with a broad, crescent-shaped white stripe over eye contrasting with reddish-brown head. Flanks are grey and there are trailing black, blue and grey feathers on back. Female is very similar to a female Teal, but slightly greyer and with a pale spot at base of bill. In flight, both sexes show a bluish forewing and green speculum. Juveniles resemble female.

KEY FACT If alarmed, the Garganey takes off steeply from the water with a rapid, direct flight, unlike the swerving flight of the Teal. The distinctive bluish wing colour of both sexes helps identification.

MALE

LOCATION	DATE/TIME

STATUS AND HABITS

The Garganey is a scarce and elusive summer visitor to Britain and Europe from overwintering grounds in tropical Africa. Favouring well-vegetated marshes and lake margins, these secretive birds can be tricky to see, and they never occur in dense concentrations. Arriving in late spring, usually in pairs or small parties, they spread out from the coast to inland breeding sites, where nests are hidden in dense tussocks of grass. They feed quietly in shallow water, using the bill to sift through plants for food.

FEMALE

SHOVELER
Anas clypeata

FACT FILE

SIZE Length 44–52cm HABITAT Shallow water, lake margins FOOD Small invertebrates, molluscs, some plant material VOICE Males make quiet *tuc* sounds; females quack

IDENTIFICATION

A distinctive broad, flattened bill makes identification of both sexes straightforward. Male has a glossy green head and bright orange belly that contrast with mostly white breast and flanks, and dark upperparts and stern. Female has mottled brown plumage and a brown bill with orange edges. In flight, both sexes show a blue forewing with a white band separating green speculum. Juveniles resemble female.

KEY FACT The strange bill of the Shoveler is ideally suited to sieving through soft mud, having a broad tip and serrated margins that allow water to escape from the sides while retaining small food items.

MALE

LOCATION	DATE/TIME

STATUS AND HABITS

Shovelers are regularly seen in winter feeding in shallow water and marshes, using their bills to sieve food from the mud as they walk slowly forwards. In the breeding season they are very secretive, choosing to nest in well-vegetated areas, but they do perform display flights over their territories. When not feeding, Shovelers may join mixed flocks of other waterbirds in open water for safety. They are present year-round in Britain, their numbers increasing in winter as migrants arrive from colder regions.

FEMALE

PINTAIL
Anas acuta

FACT FILE

SIZE Length 51–66cm HABITAT Shallow water,
marshes, lake margins FOOD Plant shoots and seeds,
invertebrates VOICE Male makes quiet whistling calls;
females make quiet quacks

IDENTIFICATION

Male is a very distinctive duck with an elegant, streamlined shape
terminating in a long, upcurved tail. Underparts are white, and a white
stripe runs up sides of chocolate-brown head. Back and flanks are grey
and black with fine vermiculations, and stern is buff and black, showing
well when bird upends to feed. Female has mostly mottled brown
plumage and a dark grey bill, but a similar streamlined shape to male.
Juveniles resemble female but with duller plumage.

KEY FACT Freezing conditions inland drive Pintails to the coast,
where they feed on tidal marshes, seeking out tiny brackish-water
molluscs and crustaceans.

MALE

LOCATION	DATE/TIME

STATUS AND HABITS

The Pintail is mainly a winter visitor to Britain, arriving in large flocks
after leaving its N breeding grounds, where it is a very nervous and
secretive bird. Here it prefers the safety of open areas, often associating
with other species of dabbling wildfowl, although it can easily be spotted
thanks to its distinctive plumage, larger size and streamlined shape.
When alarmed, Pintails take to the air with a strong and powerful
flight, looking very long-bodied in comparison with other ducks.

FEMALE

TUFTED DUCK
Aythya fuligula

FACT FILE

SIZE Length 40–47cm HABITAT Open water, lakes, wide rivers FOOD Small molluscs, aquatic invertebrates, plant material VOICE Harsh but quiet growling notes

IDENTIFICATION

Male is a distinctive black and white duck with a trailing head crest. At close range, plumage has a distinct sheen. Bill is grey with a black tip, and yellow eye contrasts with dark face. Female is mostly brown with a paler breast and flanks, and sometimes with a pale patch at base of bill. Juveniles resemble female.

KEY FACT Tufted Ducks show striking white wingbars in flight, these contrasting well with their dark plumage, and their dumpy shape and short tail give a characteristic profile.

MALE

LOCATION	DATE/TIME

STATUS AND HABITS

Tufted Ducks can be seen in Britain throughout the year, but in winter large numbers arrive from the **NE**. Diving frequently to feed, they swim well underwater in search of food. Flocks are active through the day and remain on the water to sleep at night. The birds readily take to man-made habitats such as reservoirs and gravel pits, and even live in urban parks. In the breeding season they are more secretive; females conceal their nests in deep vegetation a short way from the water.

FEMALE

GREATER SCAUP
Aythya marila

SIZE Length 42–51cm **HABITAT** Winter visitor on coasts and estuaries **FOOD** Mainly aquatic molluscs **VOICE** Usually silent, but makes harsh, grating calls in flight

IDENTIFICATION

At a glance, male Greater Scaup is similar to male Tufted Duck, but back is grey, and head shows a dark green gloss and lacks a crest. Female has mostly brown plumage with a darker head, yellow eye and large, pale patches at base of bill, forehead and cheeks. In flight, both sexes show conspicuous white wingbars. Juveniles resemble female.

KEY FACT Coastal flocks in winter consist of adults and juveniles, which keep together in family groups. Young males start to moult into adult plumage by the end of their first winter, but do not gain full adult plumage until their second winter.

MALE

LOCATION	DATE/TIME

STATUS AND HABITS

The Greater Scaup is a winter visitor to Britain from its coastal tundra
breeding grounds in Scandinavia and Iceland, arriving on our coasts in
autumn when driven SW by harsh weather. Its preferred habitat is shallow
coastal lagoons and bays where it can dive for small molluscs. When not
feeding, flocks remain on the water, bobbing in the waves, often sleeping
like this until the tide drops. Occasional birds turn up on inland lakes and
gravel pits, but they are unlikely to find sufficient food in fresh waters.

FEMALE

POCHARD
Aythya ferina

SIZE Length 42–49cm **HABITAT** Small pools and lush **FACT FILE**
lakes in summer; open water in winter **FOOD** Aquatic plants, seeds,
invertebrates **VOICE** Usually quiet, but can make harsh growling calls

IDENTIFICATION

Male is attractive and distinctive, with a chestnut-orange head and neck,
black neck and breast, and grey back and flanks. Long, broad bill is dark
with a central grey band. Females have mottled grey-brown plumage,
looking greyer on back, and a similar bill to male. Juveniles resemble
female. In flight, the wings of all birds look rather plain.

KEY FACT   Pochards are naturally wary birds, keeping away from
humans by moving out to deep water, but a few birds sometimes stray
to urban lakes, where they may become accustomed to being fed
alongside other ducks.

MALE

LOCATION	DATE/TIME

STATUS AND HABITS

In winter, Pochards gather in large flocks, often associating with Tufted Ducks, but they tend to feed more in shallow water where they can find plant roots and seeds, and are often found in well-vegetated lakes rather than large man-made reservoirs. In summer, they prefer smaller, more secluded water bodies where they can nest in thick cover. The resident population in S Britain is joined by large flocks of migrants in winter, and together they move further S if ice prevents them from feeding. They are unlikely to be seen on coastal waters.

FEMALE

RED-CRESTED POCHARD
Netta rufina

FACT FILE

SIZE Length 53–57cm HABITAT Well-vegetated freshwater lakes and marshes FOOD Plant roots, shoots and seeds VOICE Usually silent

IDENTIFICATION
Orange head and bright red bill of male are striking, contrasting with black neck and breast, brown back and white flanks. Female has more subdued colours, with mostly pale brown plumage, a dark cap and nape, white cheeks and neck, and a pink-tipped dark bill. In flight, wings of both sexes show a broad white stripe above and a pale underside. Juveniles resemble female.

KEY FACT Red-crested Pochards are resident in S Spain and have a scattered distribution across S Europe, with a few migrants breeding on lakes in central Europe in summer; some of these migrants get blown off course and arrive in Britain.

MALE

LOCATION	DATE/TIME

STATUS AND HABITS

This is a scarce bird in Britain, with a few records each year of migrants from warmer parts of Europe appearing on lakes where they can feed without disturbance. Naturally wary of humans, this is a difficult bird to observe, so any individual that can be approached closely is likely to have escaped from captivity. Red-crested Pochards prefer lakes where they can dive or dabble for plant food, and are usually seen in pairs, rarely in flocks. They are unlikely to associate freely with other wildfowl.

FEMALE

FERRUGINOUS DUCK
Aythya nyroca

SIZE Length 38–42cm **HABITAT** Rare visitor to shallow weedy lakes and pools **FOOD** Plant roots, shoots and seeds **VOICE** Usually silent, but male has whistling courtship calls and female has quiet flight calls

IDENTIFICATION

At a distance, male looks all dark brown, apart from pale eye and white stern. Grey bill has a dark tip and white band. Female is similar, but with more uniform brown plumage and a dark eye. In flight, bold white wingbar and pale underwing of both sexes are clearly seen. Juveniles resemble female but lack a white stern.

KEY FACT Not resident in Britain – any sightings here are likely to be of migrant birds getting blown off course from E Europe, although very confiding individuals are more probably escapes from captivity.

MALE

LOCATION	DATE/TIME

STATUS AND HABITS

A secretive and quiet bird, sometimes difficult to spot in its favourite habitat of dense marginal vegetation where trees and reeds overhang the water. Here, the birds' colours provide perfect camouflage, and as they spend some time diving they are easily overlooked. They are as much at home on small ponds and marshes as on larger lakes, and are usually found in pairs, rarely gathering in large flocks.

FEMALE

GOLDENEYE
Bucephala clangula

FACT FILE

SIZE **Length 42–50cm** HABITAT **Nests near forested lakes in the N; winters on coasts and large lakes** FOOD **Aquatic invertebrates** VOICE **Mostly silent, but may give croaking display calls**

IDENTIFICATION

A compact diving duck with a distinctive 'peaked' head outline. Male's head is dark glossy green with a white patch on face and a yellow eye. Body is mostly white with a dark back and stern. Female's head is reddish brown, bill is grey with a pink patch near tip, and rest of plumage is greyish brown, paler on underside. Juveniles resemble female but with a dark eye.

KEY FACT

Nests are often built in tree-holes near N lakes; birds also take readily to nestboxes, despite their extreme wariness of humans. Although they are diving ducks, they can perch in trees.

MALE

LOCATION	DATE/TIME

STATUS AND HABITS

The **Goldeneye** is most familiar as a winter visitor to Britain from its **NE** breeding grounds, when small flocks can be seen bobbing buoyantly in open water and diving frequently for food. Birds favour ice-free water bodies, spending most of their time in fresh water but moving to the coast in very cold conditions, when they may gather in bays and estuaries. In early spring, males make their head-tossing displays, and pairs migrate **N** earlier than other ducks for the breeding season.

FEMALE

RED-BREASTED MERGANSER
Mergus serrator

FACT FILE

SIZE Length 52–58cm HABITAT Breeds on upland lakes and rivers; winters mainly on coasts FOOD Fish, some aquatic invertebrates VOICE Usually silent, but may make quiet grating sounds

IDENTIFICATION

A slim, long-bodied duck with a long sawbill. Male has a red bill, legs and eyes, a glossy, dark green head with an untidy crest, a white neck collar and a speckled brown breast. Upperparts are black and white, and flanks and underside are grey with fine markings. Female has grey-brown plumage and an orange head, also with an untidy crest. In flight, wings of all birds show large white patches. Juveniles resemble female.

KEY FACT

The serrated bill is the perfect adaptation for capturing and holding onto slippery fish; Red-breasted Mergansers are good swimmers and can pursue small fish in fast-flowing rivers or the sea, sometimes bringing them to the surface before swallowing them.

MALE

LOCATION	DATE/TIME

STATUS AND HABITS

In summer, Red-breasted Mergansers are secretive birds, nesting alongside clear lakes and rivers in the far **N** of Britain, Ireland, Iceland and Scandinavia. In autumn, they migrate **S** to coasts, where they feed in sheltered bays and estuaries, sometimes venturing inland to fresh waters. By the end of the winter they start courtship, with males displaying to groups of females. In areas with plenty of fish they may be present in small flocks, but are less gregarious in summer.

FEMALE

GOOSANDER
Mergus merganser

FACT FILE

SIZE **Length 58–66cm** HABITAT **Breeds near upland lakes and rivers; winters on large lakes, rivers, reservoirs and sometimes sheltered coasts** FOOD **Fish** VOICE **Usually silent, but males produce ringing calls during courtship**

IDENTIFICATION

A large sawbill duck. Male looks black and white at a distance, but at closer range is seen to have a red bill, greenish gloss on head, pink tinge to white parts, and a greyer lower back and tail. Female is mostly mottled grey, with a reddish-brown head and white throat and neck. In flight, male shows a large white inner wing and female a white speculum. Juveniles resemble female.

KEY FACT

Goosanders are very fast and skilful swimmers, both above and below the surface. When small flocks gather they often swim in close formation, but below the water they hunt their prey alone.

MALE

LOCATION	DATE/TIME

STATUS AND HABITS

The elegant **Goosander** is mainly a winter visitor to Britain, although some birds breed near rocky rivers and lakes in the **N** and **W**, using tree-holes or nestboxes close to water. In winter, they gather where fish can easily be found, sometimes roosting at night on small ponds and then flying off to feed on larger rivers and lakes during the day. Courtship begins in early spring, when males perform elaborate dances on the water with much neck-stretching and head-bobbing.

FEMALE

SMEW
Mergus albellus

SIZE Length 38–44cm **HABITAT** Winter visitor on large lakes, sheltered coasts and estuaries **FOOD** Mainly small fish, aquatic invertebrates **VOICE** Usually silent, but male may make quiet display calls

IDENTIFICATION

A small, compact sawbill duck, with a short, serrated-edged blue-grey bill. Male has mostly white plumage, with black lines along body, around eye and on back. Head feathers have a slight tufted appearance. Flanks have fine grey markings. Female has grey-brown plumage, a reddish-brown cap and white cheeks. Immature male resembles female.

KEY FACT Winter visitors here are usually 'redheads', which are both young birds and the very similar females, and they often consort with Goldeneyes. Young males start to moult into adult plumage at the end of the winter.

MALE

LOCATION	DATE/TIME

STATUS AND HABITS

The Smew is a scarce winter visitor to Britain, favouring large, ice-free lakes and reservoirs, and sometimes sheltered coasts, where small fish are plentiful. They are very hardy birds, tolerant of cold conditions, only moving away when lakes are frozen over. Usually present in small groups or singly, they can be difficult to spot as they dive frequently and energetically. In their breeding grounds in N Russia and Scandinavia, they may use tree-holes or nestboxes near lakes.

FEMALE

RUDDY DUCK
Oxyura jamaicensis

FACT FILE

SIZE Length 35–43cm HABITAT Ponds, lakes, gravel pits with vegetated margins FOOD Mostly aquatic invertebrates, some plant material VOICE Usually silent

IDENTIFICATION

A small, compact duck with a large, broad bill and long tail. Male has mostly orange-brown plumage with a black cap, white face and bright blue bill. Moulting males retain white faces, but have dull brown plumage. Female has subdued grey-brown plumage, and a paler face with a brown bill. Both sexes have the same distinctive profile. Juveniles resemble females.

KEY FACT

Ruddy Ducks are known as 'stifftail' ducks because of their habit of raising their comparatively long tail in the air, giving them a distinctive profile. Males perform an elaborate courtship display, bobbing their heads and creating bubbles in the water.

MALE

LOCATION	DATE/TIME

STATUS AND HABITS

Introduced to wildfowl collections in Britain from North America,
Ruddy Ducks escaped into the wild in the 1950s and soon established
a breeding population here. Although they are rarely seen in flight, they
spread rapidly in Britain and beyond, and in S Europe hybridised with
the native White-headed Duck, causing serious conservation problems.
Naturally shy, they spend most time diving in shallow water for food,
but may gather in small flocks in winter, when they are easier to see.
Nests are concealed in dense vegetation.

FEMALE

MANDARIN
Aix galericulata

SIZE Length 41–49cm **HABITAT** Wooded lakes and rivers **FOOD** Plant material, small invertebrates **VOICE** Mostly silent, with some quiet croaking sounds

IDENTIFICATION

Male has a long mane of dark feathers on head, a pale crescent above eye, and radiating orange feathers on neck and breast. Orange flanks terminate in sail-like feathers at rear end. Chest and back are dark, underside is mostly white and bill is reddish with a white tip. Female is mainly grey-brown with a white spectacle around eye, white belly and large white spots on neck, breast and flanks. Juveniles resemble female but with duller markings.

KEY FACT

Mandarins nest in holes in trees, which may sometimes be quite high above the water, and take readily to nestboxes. Young birds may have to jump a considerable distance to reach the water when they are ready to leave the nest.

MALE

LOCATION	DATE/TIME

STATUS AND HABITS

The strange and distinctive Mandarin originates in E Asia and was introduced to ornamental wildfowl collections in Britain, from which many escaped and established feral breeding colonies, mainly in the S but also in S Scotland. Although it is a most conspicuous bird, it can be very difficult to locate because of its quiet habits and liking for the densely wooded margins of lakes and large rivers. When not feeding in shallow water, birds may roost in trees close to water. They are usually found in pairs, although small flocks may form at times.

FEMALE

LITTLE GREBE
Tachybaptus ruficollis

SIZE **Length 25–29cm** HABITAT **Ponds, shallow lakes, slow rivers, canals; coasts in winter** FOOD **Small fish, aquatic invertebrates** VOICE **High-pitched whinny; short, shrill calls**

IDENTIFICATION

The smallest grebe, with a compact body shape and a powderpuff tail, this often fluffed up. In clear water, the yellow-green legs and lobed feet show up. Male has a dark cap and chestnut nape in breeding season, with a green patch at base of bill. Female is more uniform brown but with a paler neck. Newly hatched young have striped plumage.

KEY FACT Most Little Grebes are sedentary, but in winter our local birds may be joined by many others from E Europe, which head W to escape freezing conditions. Ice-free water bodies are essential to their survival.

SUMMER

LOCATION	DATE/TIME

STATUS AND HABITS

Resident throughout the year in suitable water bodies, Little Grebes can be found across most of Britain and Ireland, with some birds moving to larger lakes or sheltered coasts in freezing conditions. Excellent swimmers, with the legs set well back on the body, they are rarely seen on dry land, being unable to walk easily. Their excellent buoyancy enables them to spend most of their time on the water, preening and sleeping as well as feeding. Floating weedy nests are built at the water's edge.

WINTER

GREAT CRESTED GREBE
Podiceps cristatus

FACT FILE

SIZE Length 46–51cm HABITAT Lakes, gravel pits, slow rivers; some move to coasts in winter FOOD Mainly fish, but also some aquatic invertebrates VOICE Usually silent, but some harsh staccato notes in spring

IDENTIFICATION

A streamlined waterbird with a slender neck and long, pointed bill. Adult looks mainly black and white from a distance, but closer views show a grey-brown back, white flanks, a dark cap and a pink bill. In spring, conspicuous orange, chestnut-brown and black ear tufts develop. Winter plumage is more uniform pale grey-brown. Newly hatched young are fluffy, and striped black and white.

LOCATION	DATE/TIME

KEY FACT

The species' spectacular courtship display includes head-shaking with the ear tufts and crest spread out, and the 'penguin dance'. Ritual preening and offerings of billfuls of water plants are also part of the display.

STATUS AND HABITS

Great Crested Grebes occur across a wide range of watery habitats, as long as there is a plentiful supply of fish and suitable, safe nest sites. Floating weedy nests are fixed among marginal plants and the newly hatched young are tended by both parents, often taking rides on their backs. Excellent swimmers, they are able to pursue quite large fish underwater, and only leave an area if freezing conditions prevent diving for food; they are then likely to be found on sheltered coasts.

ADULT AND YOUNG

SLAVONIAN GREBE
Podiceps auritus

SIZE Length 31–38cm **HABITAT** Breeds on weedy **FACT FILE**
pools and lakes; overwinters on sheltered coasts **FOOD** Fish
VOICE Various high-pitched calls in spring, otherwise silent

IDENTIFICATION

A striking bird in its breeding plumage, with rich brick-red flanks, a black back and head, and conspicuous bright orange ear tufts stretching back from red eye. Black bill has a white tip. Winter adults have mostly pale grey plumage, with a black cap, black down back of neck, white underside and red eye. Juveniles resemble winter adults but with dusky cheeks.

KEY FACT A few pairs of Slavonian Grebes nest in secret locations in Scotland, but the bulk of the population nests in Iceland, Scandinavia and N Europe, and then migrates S and W to coastal areas for the winter.

SUMMER

LOCATION	DATE/TIME

STATUS AND HABITS

The species' showy courtship display may be seen at breeding sites, when birds rush at each other on the water with bills filled with water weeds. Floating weedy nests are constructed on lake margins, where birds may nest colonially. This species is most familiar as a winter visitor to Britain, where it may be seen on sheltered coasts, sometimes in loose mixed flocks with other grebes. Even in rough seas Slavonian Grebes remain on the water, becoming difficult to spot because of their frequent dives.

WINTER

BLACK-NECKED GREBE
Podiceps nigricollis

FACT FILE

SIZE Length 31–38cm **HABITAT** Breeds on weedy lakes and pools, overwinters near coasts **FOOD** Fish **VOICE** Usually silent, but makes shrill, rising shrieks in courtship displays and fights

IDENTIFICATION

Similar to the Slavonian Grebe, but head is peaked and tip of bill tilts upwards, both features that can be seen in silhouette. In summer, adults have black upperparts with bright brick-red flanks. Eyes are red, with wavy tufts of orange-red feathers behind them. Winter plumage is more uniform grey, with a white underside and neck; black on head extends below eye. Juveniles resemble winter adults but with buff neck patches.

KEY FACT The Black-necked Grebe is a scarce breeding bird in Britain, with a few pairs nesting at carefully guarded lowland sites; they are joined by many more migrants from E Europe in the winter.

SUMMER

LOCATION	DATE/TIME

STATUS AND HABITS

Black-necked Grebes prefer lakes and large ponds with well-vegetated margins, where they can nest safely but also find plenty of food in open water. They are usually colonial nesters, sometimes sharing sites with terns and gulls, and outside the breeding season they may be seen in small flocks in sheltered coastal bays and estuaries. Only very rough weather will drive them inland from the sea, when they will turn up on rivers and gravel pits. They roost on the water and are more likely to swim or dive to escape danger than take to the air.

WINTER

CORMORANT
Phalacrocorax carbo

SIZE Length 80–100cm **HABITAT** Mainly coastal, but also occurs on large rivers and lakes **FOOD** Fish, especially eels and flatfish **VOICE** Usually silent, but utters deep guttural croaks at nest sites

IDENTIFICATION

A large waterbird with a bulky body, short, strong legs and feet, broad wings and a powerful bill with a hooked tip. Adult plumage is mostly dark with a scaly appearance and a green gloss in breeding season. White thigh patches develop in early spring, chin is white and bill has a yellow base. Juveniles are much browner, with extensive areas of white on underside.

KEY FACT After a session in the water, Cormorants can be seen rubbing their bill on the base of their tail to obtain oil from the preen gland, before meticulously preening each feather to maintain waterproofing.

LOCATION	DATE/TIME

STATUS AND HABITS

Cormorants are powerful birds, able to swim well in pursuit of fish on the seabed, and are often seen emerging at the surface with a wriggling eel or Flounder. After a fishing session they are commonly seen perching near the water with wings outstretched. Despite having webbed feet they are able to perch in trees, where they sometimes nest, but cliffs are their favoured sites, and they may form large colonies. Cormorants are increasingly frequent on inland water bodies like reservoirs, sometimes roosting on pylons.

GREY HERON
Ardea cinerea

SIZE Length 90–98cm HABITAT Wide range of
wetlands, sometimes on coasts FOOD Fish, amphibians, invertebrates
VOICE Harsh *crank* call, otherwise silent

FACT FILE

IDENTIFICATION
Adult plumage is mostly grey on back and white on underside, with black
areas on neck, head and 'shoulders'. A trailing crest of black feathers is
usually present. Long legs and large feet are yellowish green, and dagger-
shaped bill is large and yellow. Juveniles have more mottled grey plumage
and a greyer bill.

LOCATION	DATE/TIME

STATUS AND HABITS

The typical pose of the **Grey Heron** is standing motionless in shallow water, bill poised ready to strike if prey comes close enough. Sometimes birds stalk slowly through the shallows, hoping to dislodge prey with their long toes. After feeding, Grey Herons normally preen themselves thoroughly, using the powdery feathers on the chest to help remove slime. Nests are built high in trees, often colonially, and breeding commences early in the year. A widespread bird, found in a wide range of freshwater habitats, the Grey Heron will move to the coast in large numbers in freezing conditions.

KEY FACT

Grey Herons present a large outline when in flight, with huge, broad wings and slow, powerful wingbeats. The neck is kinked and the head drawn back to the body, but the legs trail behind.

BITTERN
Botaurus stellaris

FACT FILE

SIZE Length 70–80cm HABITAT Reedbeds; may be forced to more open areas in freezing conditions FOOD Mostly fish, plus some other aquatic life VOICE Male makes deep booming calls in spring, otherwise silent

KEY FACT When alarmed, the Bittern will freeze in one position with head and neck stretched upwards, its remarkable camouflage making it extremely difficult to spot. Even when it moves, it takes very slow, deliberate steps.

IDENTIFICATION

A large heron-like bird. Adult has mottled buff-brown plumage, showing darker bars, streaks and arrow-shaped spots. Head and neck are dark with darker moustachial stripes. Legs and feet are yellowish green, and large, dagger-shaped bill is yellowish. Long neck is often hunched up when resting. In flight, broad wings give an owl-like profile; head and neck are tucked in but legs and feet trail behind. Juveniles resemble adults but with browner head markings.

LOCATION	DATE/TIME

STATUS AND HABITS

Bitterns are more likely to be heard than seen, as the male's far-carrying, booming call can be heard at a distance of 5km on spring evenings. Glimpses of a bird flying low over a reedbed, then dropping quickly out of sight, are the best that can be seen of this very secretive species, superbly well adapted to life in dense reeds. In winter, Bitterns may be easier to spot as they feed at the edge of ice-free reeds, and migrants may arrive from Europe.

SPOONBILL
Platalea leucorodia

FACT FILE

SIZE Length 80–90cm HABITAT Shallow lakes, coastal lagoons and estuaries FOOD Small aquatic invertebrates, tiny fish VOICE Usually silent, but may make grunting calls at nest

IDENTIFICATION

An all-white egret-like bird that often rests with its bill tucked in, making distant identification tricky. Distinctive long, flattened bill with a spoon-shaped tip and side-to-side sweeping movement through mud to feed are unique to Spoonbill. Adult plumage is all white but may look stained. In breeding season, has buffish yellow on breast and long plumes on nape. Legs and bill are black. Juveniles resemble adults but with black tips to outer primaries.

LOCATION	DATE/TIME

STATUS AND HABITS

Spoonbills are restricted to shallow lakes and lagoons where they can feed in soft, invertebrate-rich mud; they are unable to feed in freezing conditions. Small groups occasionally arrive in Britain from scattered European colonies and a few stay to breed, nesting colonially in trees and reedbeds. After feeding, small flocks are sometimes seen flying off to roost, their long necks and bills stretched out in front, with feet trailing behind.

KEY FACT

Drainage of marshes, use of pesticides and disturbance at nesting sites have reduced the numbers of Spoonbills in Europe, but they can migrate over long distances and have recently colonised E England.

LITTLE EGRET
Egretta garzetta

FACT FILE

SIZE **Length 55–65cm** HABITAT **Shallow lakes and marshes, coastal lagoons, estuaries** FOOD **Fish, amphibians, aquatic invertebrates** VOICE **Mostly silent, but makes harsh *kraah* calls at breeding colonies**

IDENTIFICATION

A pure white heron-like bird with a long, pointed black bill, black legs and bright yellow feet with long toes. In breeding season, bare skin at base of bill becomes yellow and long, elegant head plumes develop. In flight, head and neck are hunched up but legs trail behind and wings show a broad outline.

LOCATION	DATE/TIME

STATUS AND HABITS

The Little Egret is widespread across **S** Britain and Ireland, and occurs in any freshwater habitats that provide shallow water for wading and trees nearby for nesting. When hunched up in the resting position, it is not an elegant bird, but when stalking prey it is very striking. It may wait, motionless for prey to swim by, or walk slowly, pushing its long toes through mud or weed to dislodge a fish, stabbing rapidly to capture it.

Often solitary when feeding, Little Egrets usually nest in large colonies.

KEY FACT

Little Egrets were once hunted for their long white head plumes, which were used by the millinery trade, but this practice was banned and the birds are now increasingly common throughout their range.

OSPREY
Pandion haliaetus

FACT FILE

SIZE Wingspan 145–160cm HABITAT Large rivers
and lakes; coasts on migration FOOD Fish
VOICE Shrill yelps and piping calls

IDENTIFICATION

A large, long-winged bird of prey. Male looks very pale below, but wings
show a bold pattern with dark primaries and carpal patches, and there is
a dark stripe through eye. Upperparts are mostly dark brown. Tail has a
broad terminal band, and up to four narrower bands. Female and juveniles
are similar but with a dark breast-band.

KEY FACT The powerful talons of the Osprey are specially
adapted to hold onto slippery fish, having sharp, spiny claws of equal
length that can both pierce and grip the prey.

LOCATION	DATE/TIME

STATUS AND HABITS

In distant silhouette, a flying Osprey may resemble a large gull, but when fish prey is seen it hovers with deep, strong wingbeats, then dives at high speed – even disappearing underwater – before emerging with its catch. The fish is then manoeuvred head-forwards and carried off to the nest or a perch for feeding. Large, moss-lined nests of branches are built in trees, sometimes away from the water, where two to three young are reared. This is one of the most widespread birds of prey in the world.

MARSH HARRIER
Circus aeruginosus

SIZE Wingspan 115–130cm **HABITAT** Reedbeds, marshes, adjoining grasslands **FOOD** Small mammals, birds, amphibians **VOICE** Mournful, shrill *kweeooo* calls

IDENTIFICATION

A large bird of prey with relatively long wings and tail. Male has a dark brown back and wing coverts, and contrasting blue-grey back and tail. From below, markings appear more uniform but black wingtips show well. Female is mostly uniform chocolate brown above with a pale buff crown, forehead and leading edge to inner wing. Juveniles resemble female.

MALE

FEMALE

LOCATION	DATE/TIME

STATUS AND HABITS

The Marsh Harrier is sometimes spotted perched on an isolated post, but more often seen gliding effortlessly with wings outstretched and feet dangling. If it finds prey, it may make a sudden twist or turn and drop on it quickly, before flying off to feed. Nests are built of twigs and reeds on the ground deep in a reedbed; the male may bring food to the female, which will fly up to meet him and turn upside down to take the prey from his talons.

KEY FACT

Marsh Harriers normally fly low over the ground, especially when hunting, but during courtship in springtime the male may soar very high over his territory and perform spectacular stooping display flights.

KESTREL
Falco tinnunculus

SIZE **Wingspan 65–75cm** HABITAT **Open country,**
heaths, towns, roadsides FOOD **Small mammals, some birds,**
amphibians, insects VOICE **Shrill *kee-kee-kee* calls, often near nest site**

IDENTIFICATION

A small bird of prey, often seen hovering, showing its long tail, downturned
head and narrow wings. Male has a grey tail and head, brick-red spotted
upperparts and a paler spotted underside. Female is more uniform in
colour, with heavily spotted light chestnut plumage and a barred tail.
At a distance, both sexes can appear similar. Juveniles resemble female.

KEY FACT Excellent eyesight enables Kestrels to hunt well into
the dusk or in poor weather, in conditions when other birds of prey
would have to give up.

MALE

LOCATION	DATE/TIME

STATUS AND HABITS

The Kestrel is one of our commonest birds of prey, seen in a wide range of open habitats, but especially grasslands, marshes and wet meadows where small mammals are common. Its ability to hover for prolonged spells enables it to hunt prey in the open; it drops rapidly when food is spotted and then flies off to a perch to eat it. Apart from hovering, Kestrels will also stalk food such as earthworms on the ground, or sit, in their characteristic upright posture, on posts or wires to look for prey.

FEMALE

WATER RAIL
Rallus aquaticus

SIZE Length 22–28cm HABITAT Reedbeds, marshes, weedy river banks and ditches FOOD Aquatic invertebrates, insects, some plant material VOICE *Kipp kipp* calls at night; harsh squeals at other times

FACT FILE

IDENTIFICATION

Adult plumage is mostly mottled dark brown above, with an unspotted slate-grey face, neck and underside. Flanks are strongly barred and tail is white below. Slender, slightly downcurved bill is red, and legs are flesh-coloured. Sexes are similar but female is slightly smaller and has a shorter bill. Juveniles have a brown bill and are browner below.

LOCATION	DATE/TIME

STATUS AND HABITS

A very secretive bird, more often heard than seen, the **Water Rail** usually remains well hidden in reedbeds, where its slim profile enables it to move easily between the stems. Long toes help it walk on floating stems and soft mud. Occasionally, birds will move out into the open to feed or bask briefly in the sun, and freezing weather may make them move to open areas. When alarmed, they can remain motionless or flee at great speed. When the bird walks, the tail is constantly flicked up and down.

KEY FACT

Many Water Rails migrate over long distances to flee cold weather, and these birds sometimes turn up in unlikely locations such as rocky offshore islands, where they may be forced to feed in the open.

SPOTTED CRAKE
Porzana porzana

SIZE Length 22–24cm HABITAT Dense waterside vegetation, sedges and rushes FOOD Small aquatic invertebrates, seeds, shoots VOICE Far-carrying *hwitt hwitt* call, likened to the sound of a dripping tap

IDENTIFICATION

Tiny, compact waterbird. Male looks dark greyish brown at distance but shows heavily spotted plumage in good light. Tail is pale buff below and there is some barring on flanks. Legs are olive-green, and short, pointed bill is red at base but yellowish at tip. Female and juveniles are similar, but with more spots rather than bars, and less grey on underside.

KEY FACT

A scarce visitor to Britain, Spotted Crakes are most likely to be seen on migration. They come to Europe in the spring to breed, but head far to the S for the winter.

JUVENILE

LOCATION	DATE/TIME

STATUS AND HABITS

A solitary and secretive bird, the Spotted Crake is very difficult to observe in dense vegetation but can sometimes be located by its distinctive call. Nests are hidden in thick vegetation close to water and the young are rarely seen until they reach adult size, when they may be spotted emerging onto mud to feed or climbing around in bankside vegetation. Birds may also wander into damp tussocky meadows, creeping quietly through vegetation to avoid being seen. They have been observed following regular feeding circuits around ponds.

JUVENILE

MOORHEN
Gallinula chloropus

SIZE Length 32–35cm **HABITAT** Ponds, lake margins, river banks, ditches, urban parks **FOOD** Aquatic and terrestrial invertebrates, seeds, shoots **VOICE** Variety of loud contact notes, including sharp *kreck* and *kipp kipp kipp* sounds

IDENTIFICATION
Adults appear all black at a distance, but in good light back is seen to be very dark brown, underside is dark slate grey, and there is a horizontal white line on flanks and white under constantly flicked tail. Most noticeable is the shiny red shield on face and yellow-tipped bill. Juveniles are much browner, with paler flanks and white chin and throat.

LOCATION	DATE/TIME

STATUS AND HABITS

Moorhens are very well adapted to most freshwater habitats, seeming equally at home in urban parks and remote lakes and rivers. Able to swim, dabble in mud and climb through riverside trees, they are able to exploit many sources of food, including begging scraps from humans. Powerful flight enables them to reach new habitats easily. Although rather solitary and secretive in the breeding season, nesting in dense vegetation, they are more gregarious at other times, often feeding in flocks.

KEY FACT

Although most Moorhens are sedentary, N breeders undertake long migrations in winter to avoid iced-up water, forming large flocks alongside resident birds further S.

ADULTS FIGHTING

COOT
Fulica atra

SIZE **Length 36–38cm** HABITAT **Large ponds and lakes, canals, urban parks** FOOD **Mainly water plants, plus some invertebrates** VOICE **Loud, repeated *kwok* calls and piercing *pitt***

IDENTIFICATION

A plump waterbird. Adults are charcoal black with a red eye and pure white facial shield and bill. Feet have lobed toes to aid swimming. In good light at close range, head is darkest and flanks appear lighter grey. Sexes are very similar but males are larger. Juveniles are paler grey with light undersides.

KEY FACT
Coots are resident in Britain, but large numbers migrate here from the E in cold winters, forming noisy flocks and often mixing with other diving waterfowl.

LOCATION	DATE/TIME

STATUS AND HABITS

Coots are aggressive birds, defending their territories against all intruders, often by charging across the water surface with wings held forwards. When swimming normally, the head is gently nodded. Coots dive for food with a small jump, bobbing up again nearby. Nests are often built over water among overhanging branches, and the young are tended by both parents. Avoiding very fast-flowing water, they are most at home in slow-flowing weedy rivers and canals. Birds soon become confident in urban parks, scavenging for scraps in the open.

COMMON CRANE
Grus grus

SIZE Length 110–130cm HABITAT Marshes,
farmland FOOD Fruits, seeds, roots, soil invertebrates
VOICE Far-carrying loud, bugling calls; *kroo-krii* calls between pairs

FACT FILE

IDENTIFICATION

A large bird that walks in a stately, upright manner on the ground. Adult plumage looks all grey at a distance, but head is dark with a white band down neck, eye and crown are red, legs are black and bill is pale. Chest and back have a reddish tinge. Longer wing feathers form a 'cloak' that overhangs tail. Juveniles are paler, with a plain head and grey legs.

KEY FACT Despite their similar bill, Common Cranes are not fish-eaters like Grey Herons, feeding mainly on plant material instead. In the breeding season, however, some frogs, worms, beetles and small mammals may be taken.

LOCATION	DATE/TIME

STATUS AND HABITS

Solitary and nervous in the breeding
season, Common Cranes nest on the
ground in isolated marshes and forest
clearings, mainly in Scandinavia and
N Europe, although a few pairs have
bred in Norfolk and some have been
introduced to Somerset. Wetlands
and farmland provide plenty of food,
which the birds find by stalking
slowly. In autumn, they migrate S
in noisy V-formation in family groups
that gather into larger flocks. On
their return in spring, the elaborate
courtship 'dance' may be seen,
involving much jumping, head-pointing
and wing-flapping, often performed
collectively. They are most often seen
in Britain on migration, when they
use regular stop-over sites.

OYSTERCATCHER
Haematopus ostralegus

SIZE Length 40–45cm **HABITAT** Rocky shores, estuaries, stony riverbeds and lake shores **FOOD** Molluscs, marine worms, earthworms **VOICE** Loud *kubeek kubeek* alarm notes; shrill piping calls

FACT FILE

IDENTIFICATION

A large wading bird. Adults have striking black and white plumage, a red eye, a long orange-red bill and pinkish legs. Wings show a bold white wingbar in flight. In winter, a white chin stripe appears on black neck. Newly hatched chicks have excellent camouflage, resembling mossy rocks. Juvenile birds are paler than adults with more white on chin.

SUMMER

LOCATION	DATE/TIME

WINTER

KEY FACT

Males may gather in small groups in spring and perform a strange display, calling loudly and making a variety of clapping sounds with their heads pointing downwards.

STATUS AND HABITS

Familiar as coastal birds, often roosting in large flocks at high tide, Oystercatchers are also found far inland nesting along stony riverbeds, islands in gravel pits or around large lakes, and feeding in damp ground in open fields, golf courses and marshes. Their loud calls can be heard night and day as they aggressively chase predators. The long bill enables them to probe damp ground for earthworms and invertebrates. Inland birds will migrate a short distance to nearby coastal areas in the winter.

AVOCET
Recurvirostra avosetta

FACT FILE

SIZE Length 42–46cm HABITAT Shallow lakes, marshes, coastal lagoons, estuaries FOOD Small aquatic invertebrates VOICE Various shrill calls, including a piping *pleet pleet*

IDENTIFICATION

A very distinctive large black and white wader with a slender, upcurved bill and long blue-grey legs. Adult plumage is mostly pure white with a black head and nape, and black patches on wing that have an oval shape in flight. From below, Avocets look mostly white, apart from black wingtips. Juveniles resemble adults but have a brownish head and nape.

KEY FACT Avocets are excellent parents, tending their young carefully and guiding them to the best feeding areas. They will aggressively chase off predators such as gulls and corvids.

LOCATION	DATE/TIME

STATUS AND HABITS

The characteristic feeding behaviour of the Avocet is to sweep its bill from side to side through liquid mud to catch tiny invertebrates. The long legs enable it to wade easily, but it can also upend itself like a duck in deeper water to reach the best feeding areas. Nests are built colonially on shingle banks close to good feeding areas, and are usually lined with shells or small stones. After the breeding season, most Avocets migrate to sheltered estuaries and bays where mud remains ice-free. In favoured sites winter flocks of Avocets may number hundreds of birds.

LAPWING
Vanellus vanellus

FACT FILE

SIZE Length 28–31cm HABITAT Marshes, wet grasslands, farmland pastures FOOD Soil invertebrates, especially earthworms, beetles, larvae VOICE Shrill *peeoo-wit* calls; various contact notes

IDENTIFICATION

Once known as the Green Plover, the Lapwing has glossy green upperparts, an all-white underside and orange undertail coverts, shown clearly when head is lowered for feeding and tail is raised. Both sexes have a long crest and are similar, but in spring male has a black chin and throat. In flight, the broad wings have a rounded profile and show bold black and white patterning. Winter adults have pale margins to feathers, giving a scalloped effect to back and wings. Juveniles are similar but with a browner chest and shorter crest.

LOCATION	DATE/TIME

STATUS AND HABITS

Lapwings perform acrobatic aerial displays over their breeding sites in spring, with energetic diving and swooping, accompanied by the far-carrying *peeoo-wit* calls. This manoeuvrability can also help outwit predators, and Lapwings vigorously defend their young against intruders. Open fields and grassland are favoured nesting sites, sometimes well away from water. In winter, Lapwings gather in larger flocks, some moving to the coast.

KEY FACT

Damper areas provide the best feeding for Lapwings, and birds will often feed at night when invertebrates are more active.

GOLDEN PLOVER
Pluvialis apricaria

FACT FILE

SIZE **Length 26–29cm** HABITAT **Breeds on upland bogs and moorland, winters on lowland pastures** FOOD **Soil invertebrates, some fruits and seeds** VOICE **Plaintive, whistling** *pyuuh-pu* **calls**

IDENTIFICATION

A medium-sized, plump wader with a rounded head, short bill and dark legs. Adult winter plumage is spangled golden brown above and pale below. Breeding male has a black face and black underside edged with white. Breeding female is similar but with less black and a greyer face. Juveniles resemble winter adults but may show faint barring below.

JUVENILE

LOCATION	DATE/TIME

STATUS AND HABITS

Golden Plovers prefer to feed on short, damp grassland where they can run around in pursuit of insects and earthworms. Their excellent camouflage enables them to feed and nest safely on the ground, and they take flight only if approached closely. Scattered pairs nest on open moorland and upland grassland, but birds gather in larger flocks in autumn to move to favoured overwintering areas – sometimes joining with Lapwings – on grass airfields and grazing marshes. Occasionally, in extreme weather, they move to coastal areas.

KEY FACT

The plain white underwing shows clearly in flight and is a good identification feature for separating the Golden Plover from the very similar Grey Plover, which has a black underwing.

WINTER

LITTLE RINGED PLOVER
Charadrius dubius

SIZE Length 14–15cm **HABITAT** Large stony
riverbeds, lake shores, gravel pits **FOOD** Aquatic invertebrates,
insects, spiders **VOICE** Mournful-sounding *kree-u kree-u* and shrill
kiu flight calls

IDENTIFICATION

A small, well-camouflaged wader. Adults have dull sandy-brown upperparts,
a pure white underside and a boldly patterned black and white head.
Black eye is surrounded by a bright yellow eye-ring. Bill is black and legs
are a dull flesh colour. In flight, wings look plain, lacking any wingbar.
Juveniles look like faded versions of adults.

LOCATION	DATE/TIME

KEY FACT If disturbed by a predator, a nesting bird will perform an elaborate and convincing wing-dragging or feeding display in order to distract attention away from its eggs or chicks.

STATUS AND HABITS

Little Ringed Plovers arrive in early spring from overwintering sites in Africa. Touching down on coasts first, they move inland to gravel pits, riverbeds and lakes, where they become very secretive as they start breeding, revealing their presence only by their plaintive calls. They have adapted well to activities such as gravel extraction and reservoir construction, readily taking to man-made sites. They avoid dense vegetation and very wet marshland, preferring stony open sites in the S.

LITTLE STINT
Calidris minuta

FACT FILE

SIZE Length 12–14cm HABITAT Winter visitor on marshes and lake shores FOOD Aquatic invertebrates in winter VOICE Thin, piping *svee svee svee* display calls; quiet *tip* contact notes

IDENTIFICATION

A very small wader with a short black bill and legs. Adult winter plumage is mostly grey-buff above and white below, but in summer upperparts are rusty red, crown is darker and cheeks are reddish. Upper feathers have dark centres and pale margins. Juveniles resemble adults but show a white 'V' pattern on upperparts.

KEY FACT

This is the smallest European sandpiper, so can be distinguished by size, but beware confusion with the only slightly larger Temminck's Stint, which also stops off here on migration.

SUMMER

LOCATION	DATE/TIME

STATUS AND HABITS

This diminutive wader often feeds among other small species like the Dunlin, but is less likely to enter the water and is usually a more active feeder, scurrying around in search of moving prey, which it captures with quick stabs of its bill. It prefers to feed in quiet backwaters and creeks, avoiding more open sites. As a passage migrant, it is most likely to be seen in spring and autumn, and only in ones and twos, never in large flocks.

SUMMER

TEMMINCK'S STINT
Calidris temminckii

FACT FILE

SIZE Length 13–15cm HABITAT Winter visitor on inland marshes; nests on tundra FOOD Small insects, worms, tiny molluscs VOICE High, ringing *tirrr*

IDENTIFICATION
Very small wader with a short, very slightly downcurved bill, short legs and a proportionately long tail. Winter adults have greyish-brown plumage above and mostly white underparts but with a distinct grey chest, more clearly defined than in Little Stint. Breeding birds show more colour above, with some feathers having dark centres and reddish edges. Juveniles have a scaly appearance owing to pale edges of larger feathers.

KEY FACT If startled by a predator, Temminck's Stints will fly rapidly upwards, sometimes giving a brief alarm call, and then head off with an erratic flight path for some distance before settling down again.

SUMMER

LOCATION	DATE/TIME

STATUS AND HABITS

Temminck's Stints breed in the tundra of **NW Scandinavia, N Russia** and **N Siberia**, although a few pairs have bred in the **Scottish Highlands**. Pairs choose damp grassy areas with small clumps of willow scrub nearby as nesting areas. They like to have tree stumps or rocks as lookout points and shallow pools for feeding. They sometimes migrate in small parties, stopping off at small pools and marshes. Most of the European population migrates overland to overwinter around the **E Mediterranean** coastline.

WINTER

DUNLIN
Calidris alpina

SIZE Length 16–22cm **HABITAT** Breeds on
moorlands and tundra; overwinters on sandy shores and lakes
FOOD Insects in summer; small invertebrates in winter
VOICE Trilling display calls over nest sites; harsh *krreee* in flight

IDENTIFICATION

A small wader, winter adults with mostly grey-brown plumage above and
a pale underside. Summer adults have slightly browner upperparts and
belly is black. In flight, a distinct white wingbar can be seen. All Dunlin
have a slightly downcurved black bill, but its length varies according to
race. Juveniles resemble moulting adults but breast is streaked and
upperparts are paler owing to buff margins to feathers.

SUMMER

LOCATION	DATE/TIME

STATUS AND HABITS

The Dunlin is one of the commonest waders to be seen in winter in Britain, but many are also present here in summer, nesting on moors and uplands. In winter they migrate to coasts and marshes, joined by birds from further N. In the breeding season they tend to be solitary and secretive, revealing their presence only by the male's trilling display calls. In winter they congregate in large flocks, often flying in formation, wheeling and turning together, the flocks changing colour from grey to white.

KEY FACT Dunlin that breed in Britain and Ireland have a slightly shorter bill and smaller black belly patch than birds from elsewhere in Europe, and can usually be picked out in mixed flocks.

WINTER

CURLEW SANDPIPER
Calidris ferruginea

FACT FILE

SIZE Length 18–20cm HABITAT Passage migrant, stopping off on coasts and marshes FOOD Insects on breeding grounds; shrimps, worms, tiny molluscs in winter VOICE *Krillee* flight calls, otherwise silent

IDENTIFICATION

In summer plumage adults are striking, with a rich red underside and darker mottled upperparts. Newly moulted plumage has a mealy appearance owing to unworn pale feather margins. Bill is black and downcurved, legs are relatively long and black, and white rump patch and pale wingbar show in flight. Juveniles have much paler buff-orange upperparts and chest, pale underside and pale eye-stripe.

KEY FACT Curlew Sandpipers have the ability to deposit body fat very quickly, so a few days' non-stop feeding on tiny invertebrates will provide enough reserves for the next stage of a long migration.

SUMMER

LOCATION	DATE/TIME

STATUS AND HABITS

Curlew Sandpipers make long migrations from overwintering sites in tropical Africa to their Arctic breeding grounds, and a few birds may stop off in spring on coasts and marshes in the E Mediterranean or even in Britain. They are more likely seen here on return migration in autumn, when some take a more **W** route. At this time they sometimes join with Dunlin, when they can be picked out by their larger size and longer, more curved bill; many of these birds will be juveniles with paler plumage.

SPRING

GREENSHANK
Tringa nebularia

FACT FILE

SIZE Length 30–35cm HABITAT Breeds on bogs, marshes; overwinters on coasts, lakes, marshes FOOD Aquatic and terrestrial invertebrates, tiny fish, tadpoles VOICE Clear, three-note *chew-chew-chew* calls

IDENTIFICATION

Looking grey and white from a distance, adult **Greenshanks** in breeding plumage have darker markings on upperparts and arrow-shaped markings on chest, giving them a streaked appearance. In winter, underside is pure white, and upperparts have a slightly scaly appearance owing to paler feather margins. Juveniles resemble winter adults, but with browner plumage and more defined streaks on neck and breast.

KEY FACT In flight, the Greenshank's wings look all dark with no wingbars, but there is a narrow, pale rump patch that extends along the back, and the very pale tail shows some faint barring.

JUVENILE

LOCATION	DATE/TIME

STATUS AND HABITS

The **Greenshank** is a scarce breeding bird in **N S**cotland, but a frequent passage migrant in autumn and a regular winter visitor to coasts and marshes. Usually fairly solitary, it prefers sheltered creeks and backwaters, and small marshy pools where it can hunt prey such as small fish. Running through the shallows with the slightly upcurved bill held underwater is a favourite method of catching small fish like sticklebacks, which are lifted out of the water before being swallowed.

SUMMER

REDSHANK
Tringa totanus

SIZE **Length** 27–29cm HABITAT **Wet meadows, marshes, estuaries, sheltered coasts** FOOD **Insect larvae, earthworms, marine invertebrates** VOICE **Two-note *tu-hu* call; *tyoo tyoo tyoo* flight call; louder *klu-klu-klu* alarm call**

IDENTIFICATION

All plumages have long orange-red legs and a reddish base to long bill. In winter, adults are mostly grey-brown above and pale below, but in breeding season upperparts become darker with browner patches in feathers, N birds being darker than those from the S. Juveniles are similar to adults but legs are dull orange and underside has a slightly barred appearance.

KEY FACT In flight in all plumages, the wings look darker at the tip and outer edges and show a white trailing edge, and juveniles resemble adults.

BREEDING

SPOTTER'S CHART

LOCATION	DATE/TIME

STATUS AND HABITS

In the breeding season, the male Redshank will display by rising and falling on rapid wingbeats, giving a far-carrying tyoo tyoo tyoo flight call. When landing, he stands briefly with wings raised, showing the pure white underside. Birds also gives a shrill alarm call at any sign of danger, meriting their old name of Warden of the Marshes. Nests are built in clumps of grass, and newly hatched young are tended by both parents. After the breeding season most birds migrate to the coast.

WINTER

SPOTTED REDSHANK
Tringa erythropus

FACT FILE

SIZE **Length 29–32cm** HABITAT **Passage migrant; rare winter visitor to estuaries and marshes** FOOD **Small invertebrates, both terrestrial and aquatic** VOICE **Repetitive, whirring *kruu-ee* display calls; shrill *chu-witt* flight calls**

IDENTIFICATION
An elegant wader with long red legs and a long bill. Breeding adults are mostly sooty black with pale margins to feathers on upperparts (these give rise to its common name), and bill and legs are brighter red in summer. Winter birds are pale grey-brown above and white below. Juveniles resemble winter adults but with grey barring below.

KEY FACT In flight, Spotted Redshanks show a narrow, wedge-shaped white rump patch, but no wingbar, easily distinguishing them from the similar Redshank. Their shrill call also differs from that of the Redshank.

PARTIAL BREEDING

LOCATION	DATE/TIME

STATUS AND HABITS

Spotted Redshanks nest in Arctic bogs and tundra, with the males helping with every stage of rearing young, including incubation. Females leave the breeding areas long before males. Feeding in shallow water, often in small groups, they make distinctive downwards stabbing movements with their long bill, sometimes venturing into quite deep water and upending like ducks. A few overwinter here on marshes and estuaries where they can find soft mud to feed in, often returning year after year to the same place.

WINTER

GREEN SANDPIPER
Tringa ochropus

SIZE Length 21–24cm **HABITAT** Boggy ground near trees, streams, lake shores, Watercress beds **FOOD** Mainly aquatic invertebrates, some fish fry and insects **VOICE** Shrill, three-note *tueet-wit-wit*

FACT FILE

IDENTIFICATION

From a distance, looks dark above and white below, with a dark bill and greenish legs. Summer adults have dark olive-green upperparts, speckled with white, and a greyish head. In winter, upperparts lack spots and look uniformly dark, contrasting with white underside. In flight, wings look dark with no wingbar, rump is dark, tail is barred and feet trail a short way behind tail. Juveniles have buff-brown spots on dark upperparts and a streaked neck and chest.

LOCATION	DATE/TIME

STATUS AND HABITS

Green Sandpipers will feed in areas where other waders are unlikely to occur, such as weedy farm ditches, Watercress beds and small, isolated ponds. They often fly off rapidly at the last moment, giving the distinctive trisyllabic call, before quickly dropping into cover again. Usually solitary, they will sometimes gather in winter in small groups in good feeding areas – usually freshwater sites, although freezing conditions may drive them to the coast. When not feeding they roost on small rocks or tussocks close to the water.

KEY FACT

In the breeding season Green Sandpipers look for old pigeon or thrush nests for their nesting sites, offering the unusual sight of a wader in a tree.

WOOD SANDPIPER
Tringa glareola

SIZE Length 19–21cm **HABITAT** Open forests with boggy clearings, marshes, riversides **FOOD** Aquatic and terrestrial invertebrates, tiny fish, tadpoles, seeds **VOICE** Trilling display calls on breeding sites; *jiff jiff* flight and alarm calls

IDENTIFICATION

A small, slim, relatively long-legged sandpiper. Adults have brownish-grey upperparts speckled with white and a pale underside. In flight, wings are pale below but have no wingbar above, rump is white and tail is finely barred. Breeding plumage (seen in Britain) is darker and more speckled. Juveniles have browner colours than adults, and a streaked neck, chest and flanks.

LOCATION	DATE/TIME

STATUS AND HABITS

Wood Sandpipers breed in
remote N forests of Scandinavia,
but migrate over long distances
to Africa, stopping off early
in the autumn in Britain on
marshes, flood-meadows and
muddy riversides. They usually
avoid exposed coasts and
beaches, preferring
more sheltered,
freshwater sites.
These visitors are
mostly juvenile birds
with distinct brown
tones in the plumage.
Passage migrants are
rarely seen on their
return migration in
the spring.

KEY FACT

Wood Sandpipers
may nest on the ground in dense
vegetation, or sometimes in a tree,
and there have been a few scattered
records of birds nesting in Britain,
although most individuals seen here
are migrants.

SPRING

COMMON SANDPIPER
Actitis hypoleucos

FACT FILE

SIZE Length 19–21cm HABITAT Stony rivers and lake margins; sheltered coasts in winter FOOD Aquatic insects and other invertebrates VOICE Shrill, rapid *hee dee dee* flight and alarm calls; rhythmic *will-he-wicket* display song

IDENTIFICATION

Adults look plain grey-buff above at a distance, but in fact have delicately patterned upperparts with fine markings that fade in winter. Underside is pure white with a distinct white shoulder patch. Legs are grey-green, and short bill is dark brown with a hint of yellow at base. Juveniles have a scaly appearance, resulting from pale feather margins.

KEY FACT

When disturbed, the Common Sandpiper will fly off low over the water, almost touching it with its wings, and give its shrill alarm call. The dark wings show a narrow white bar.

LOCATION	DATE/TIME

STATUS AND HABITS

The Common Sandpiper is a widespread resident wader, found in a great range of freshwater habitats across Britain and Europe. It usually feeds actively at the edge of a lake or river, constantly bobbing up and down and making short dashes after prey, which it stabs swiftly with its bill. Nests are built on the ground near water and newly hatched young are taken to water to be fed. In winter, there is a general migration S, but some birds remain near the breeding sites.

CURLEW
Numenius arquata

SIZE Length 50–60cm **HABITAT** Upland moors and bogs in breeding season; coasts and marshes in winter
FOOD Earthworms, soil invertebrates, molluscs, crustaceans on coasts
VOICE Mournful *cour-lee* calls; bubbling trill on breeding sites

IDENTIFICATION
A large wader with a long, downcurved bill, longer in female, which is also a larger bird; otherwise, sexes are similar. Both have mottled brown plumage and paler undersides. In summer, plumage has a more yellow tone than in winter and bill is all dark. In winter, lower mandible is pinkish brown. Juveniles resemble winter adults.

LOCATION	DATE/TIME

STATUS AND HABITS

The unmistakable ringing call of the Curlew is as evocative of wild bogs and marshes in spring as it is of estuaries and wetlands in winter. In the

breeding season birds will be fairly solitary and secretive, nesting in tussocks on bogs and guarding their chicks until they can fly. In autumn they gather in large flocks and move to marshes and coasts, where they feed in muddy areas on a wide range of invertebrates. They are vocal through the year, calling in flight and on the ground.

KEY FACT The long, curved bill of the Curlew is the perfect implement for probing soft mud and extracting burrowing prey. The birds are also adept at removing the soft bodies of molluscs from their shells.

BLACK-TAILED GODWIT
Limosa limosa

SIZE Length 36–44cm **HABITAT** Breeds on damp meadows and marshes; overwinters on sheltered coasts and wetlands **FOOD** Invertebrates, caught by probing in soft mud **VOICE** Usually quiet, but on nest site gives rapid, nasal *kee wee wee wee* calls

IDENTIFICATION

A large wader with long legs and a long, straight bill. In breeding plumage, head and neck are brick red, and chest and upperparts are mottled with black, chestnut and grey, giving appearance of broken dark bars, especially on upper chest. Underside is mostly pale grey. Winter birds are pale grey above and white below. Juveniles have more brown-buff tones.

KEY FACT The amount of red on the head and neck is variable, with some birds very pale in summer, but all show a half black and half white tail, and bold white wingbars.

SUMMER

LOCATION	DATE/TIME

STATUS AND HABITS

Freshwater marshes, especially if grazed by cattle and intersected by ditches, are favoured breeding sites for **Black-tailed Godwits**, and they often nest semi-colonially. Once they are large enough, young birds are taken to muddy lake shores or estuaries, where the feeding is more productive. Long legs enable the birds to wade in quite deep water, and the long bill can probe to depths that other waders cannot reach. The tip of the bill is sensitive and also slightly flexible, allowing the bird to detect prey and extract it from the mud.

WINTER

RUFF
Philomachus pugnax

FACT FILE

SIZE Length 26–32cm **HABITAT** Wet meadows, marshes, swamps, muddy lake margins, sheltered coastal lagoons
FOOD Variety of invertebrates from the soil and water margins
VOICE Usually silent, but may make quiet squeaks

IDENTIFICATION

An unusual wader with great variations in plumage. Winter plumage of both sexes is mostly mottled brownish buff above, buff on chest and pale below. Dark bill is slightly downcurved and legs are reddish. Breeding male has elaborate head and neck feathers, which fluff out to form a *ruff*; these vary between individuals. Breeding female is smaller than male, and has mostly buff upperparts with variable mottling and streaking, and a paler underside. Juveniles resemble winter adults but with more buff colours.

FEMALE

LOCATION	DATE/TIME
--	-----------
--	-----------
--	-----------
--	-----------

STATUS AND HABITS

In spring, male Ruffs gather in leks near their nesting sites and strut around displaying their colourful breeding plumage, each male trying to outdo the others with its appearance and its elaborate dance, leaping into the air, or sometimes freezing in one position to show its colours to best effect. The much plainer and smaller females watch closely. Nesting semi-colonially, pairs choose large freshwater marshes as breeding sites. By late summer the males have moulted in to their more uniform winter plumage.

MALE

KEY FACT

In autumn, flocks made up mostly of juveniles gather on coastal marshes before heading to Africa for the winter. On their return migration in spring, some males may already be showing their breeding colours.

RED-NECKED PHALAROPE
Phalaropus lobatus

FACT FILE

SIZE Length 18–19cm HABITAT Breeds on small pools on open tundra, very rarely in far N Britain; winters at sea in the tropics FOOD Small invertebrates, taken while swimming; mainly insects in summer VOICE Quiet *kitt* and *kirritt* sounds

IDENTIFICATION

A delicate, small wader with a short, slender bill. In winter, both sexes look black and white at distance, but have ashy-grey upperparts and a white underside. In summer, female has a rusty-red neck and upper chest, white throat, slaty-grey head, and grey upperparts with buff streaks. Breeding male is similar but with less distinct coloration. Juveniles resemble summer male but with paler colours.

KEY FACT

The bird's spinning behaviour on shallow pools helps it feed by stirring up insect larvae from the mud below; sometimes, several birds will work together to increase their chances of finding food.

SUMMER FEMALE

LOCATION	DATE/TIME

STATUS AND HABITS

Its distinctive habit of swimming in search of food, often spinning round on the surface of a shallow pool, instantly distinguishes the Red-necked Phalarope from other small waders. More distinctive, however, is the species' role reversal in summer, with the females having the bright colours and leading the courtship. After egg-laying the male remains to incubate and care for the young. Nests are built in dense vegetation close

FEMALES FIGHTING

to water and the young are soon taken to water to learn to feed. Birds are most regularly seen as passage migrants in autumn.

SNIPE
Gallinago gallinago

SIZE Length 25–27cm **HABITAT** Bogs, damp meadows, upper reaches of saltmarshes **FOOD** Soil and freshwater invertebrates **VOICE** *Tic-a-tic* calls in breeding season; sneeze-like call when alarmed

IDENTIFICATION

A dumpy wader with a very long bill, brown at tip and paler at base, and dull green legs. Upperparts are brown with pale stripes, these more clearly defined on head; larger feathers have dark centres and pale margins, giving birds a scaly appearance and providing excellent camouflage. Flanks are barred and underside is greyish white. Short tail is barred, with a buff margin.

LOCATION	DATE/TIME

STATUS AND HABITS

The long bill is used to probe soft mud in a distinctive jerky action, the tip vibrating slightly to disturb and detect food, which can be sucked up without removing the bill from the mud. If alarmed, Snipe will fly off rapidly on a jerky flight path and drop quickly out of sight. They can also remain motionless for long periods, relying on camouflage for protection. In spring they are obvious by their displays, but at other times Snipe are very secretive, often seen only when flushed suddenly.

KEY FACT

In spring, males perform an exciting display flight, climbing high and then swooping down with splayed tail feathers, which create a curious bleating or drumming sound.

JACK SNIPE
Lymnocryptes minimus

SIZE Length 17–19cm HABITAT Non-breeding visitor; overwinters on lowland marshes FOOD Small soil and freshwater invertebrates VOICE Brief sneeze-like call when flushed; occasional whistling display call near nest

IDENTIFICATION

A small wader with short legs and a shorter bill than the Snipe. Three pale yellow stripes run along back, which is greenish brown and mottled, offering superb camouflage. Large feathers on back have dark centres and paler margins, and underside is mostly white. Legs and feet are greenish.

KEY FACT Normally silent, the Jack Snipe has an unusual display call, heard only in spring on its breeding grounds, which has been likened to the distant sound of galloping horses.

LOCATION	DATE/TIME

STATUS AND HABITS

The diminutive Jack Snipe is harder to see than the more sociable Snipe, preferring wet areas with some covering vegetation, and usually occurring singly rather than in small groups. Its constant tail-bobbing and crouching, and its ability to freeze, are useful identification features. If flushed it will fly off rapidly, giving a short alarm call. Its flight is less erratic than the Snipe's, and has weaker wingbeats. Birds occur on passage in autumn from their breeding grounds on boggy tundra in N Europe, but some also remain all winter in undisturbed habitats.

COMMON GULL
Larus canus

FACT FILE

SIZE Length 38–44cm HABITAT Coasts, sheltered freshwater marshes, lakes, large rivers FOOD Marine invertebrates, fish, insects, earthworms VOICE Harsh *keeoow* and mewing *gleeoo* calls

IDENTIFICATION

A medium-sized gull, pale grey above and pure white below, with yellowish-green legs and a yellow bill. Adults have black wingtips with white patches, and grey-brown flecks on head and neck in winter. Immatures show more brown in wings in their first winter and a black tail band. Bill is black at first, becoming a dull flesh colour and then yellow in second winter.

KEY FACT The Common Gull is smaller and more compact than the Herring Gull, has a dark eye with a red eye-ring, and lacks the orange spot on the bill.

WINTER

LOCATION	DATE/TIME

STATUS AND HABITS

Despite its name, this is not the commonest gull in Britain, nesting mainly in the N and dispersing in winter, when it is more widespread. Although it can feed at sea among other gulls, it is most at home on land or freshwater sites, and is skilled at capturing cranefly larvae and earthworms, often by following the plough on farmland. The Common Gull population increased in the 20th century because the species has been able to adapt to changing land use.

SUMMER

BLACK-HEADED GULL
Larus ridibundus

FACT FILE

SIZE Length 38–44cm HABITAT Sheltered coasts, lakes, marshes, urban sites, farmland FOOD Insects, earthworms, marine and freshwater invertebrates, food scraps VOICE Harsh, screeching calls, especially in nesting colonies

IDENTIFICATION
Summer adults have a chocolate-brown head, white nape, red bill with a black tip and red legs. Wings show a white leading edge in flight and black tips to primaries. In winter, adults' head is white, but with two dark smudges over and behind eye; legs and bill are paler red than in summer. Juveniles have browner areas in wings and a black terminal tail band. Bill and legs are a dark flesh colour in juveniles in first winter, becoming redder in second year.

SUMMER

LOCATION	DATE/TIME

KEY FACT

In winter, Black-headed Gulls may congregate in huge roosts at dusk, converging from a wide area and often mixing with larger gulls; their distinctive head patterning at this time of year is a useful aid to identification.

STATUS AND HABITS

A common and widespread gull, sometimes found in large colonies on inland marshes as well as coasts. As an opportunist feeder, Black-headed Gulls are able to exploit many food sources provided in urban areas and the countryside, and can be seen on rubbish tips, reservoirs, farmland and city centres. Plentiful food supplies through the year have enabled the population to increase and spread its range.

WINTER

HERRING GULL
Larus argentatus

SIZE Length 55–67cm HABITAT Coasts, city centres, large lakes, rivers, reservoirs FOOD Varied diet; often scavenges VOICE Various staccato 'chuckling' calls and drawn-out *aahhooo* calls

IDENTIFICATION

Summer adults have a silvery-grey mantle, black wingtips with white flecks and an all-white underside. Bill is yellow with an orange spot near tip of lower mandible. Yellow eye has an orange eye-ring and legs are pink. Winter adults have brown speckles on head. Juveniles are mottled brown with a dark bill in their first year, gradually acquiring adult plumage over four years.

SUMMER

KEY FACT It is likely that Herring Gulls mate for life, and pairs have been known to return to the same nesting site for 20 years in succession.

LOCATION	DATE/TIME

STATUS AND HABITS

Herring Gulls are very adaptable, tough and resilient birds that are able to exploit a wide range of habitats and food sources, and have learnt to find food in urban sites, open countryside, freshwater habitats, the coast and the open seas. Scavenging provides much of their food, but they also prey upon smaller birds, raiding nesting colonies and taking migrating birds. Showing little fear of humans, they respond to feeding opportunities in the centre of towns and will readily nest on rooftops.

WINTER

YELLOW-LEGGED GULL
Larus michahellis

FACT FILE

SIZE Length 55–67cm HABITAT Coasts, reservoirs, urban sites FOOD Fish, invertebrates, scavenged items VOICE Loud *aahooo* calls and various chuckling sounds

IDENTIFICATION

Adults are very similar to adult Herring Gulls, but legs are yellow and mantle is slightly darker grey. Bill is yellow with dark orange spot near tip, with colours more intense than in Herring Gull. In winter, head and neck lack dark mottled appearance of Herring Gull. Juveniles are brownish in first winter with dark legs, gradually acquiring adult plumage over next two years.

KEY FACT The Lesser Black-backed Gull also has yellow legs, but its mantle is much darker, and the wingtips show less white on the black tips.

LOCATION	DATE/TIME

STATUS AND HABITS

Formerly thought to be a race of the Herring Gull found mainly in the Mediterranean, the Yellow-legged Gull is now known to be a separate species, with at least three subspecies identified. It is mainly coastal in its habits, and a few birds can usually be found among other gulls at rubbish tips, reservoirs, harbours and gull roosts, where their bright yellow legs are useful identification features. Juveniles are more common in Britain than adults, but much more difficult to identify.

COMMON TERN
Sterna hirundo

FACT FILE

SIZE Length 31–35cm **HABITAT** Sheltered coasts, freshwater marshes, lakes, gravel pits **FOOD** Small fish, invertebrates **VOICE** Harsh, insistent *keey-yah* calls; various short alarm notes

IDENTIFICATION

Summer adults have mostly pale grey upperparts, a black head, and a white tail, rump and underside. Short legs are bright red and bill is red with a dark tip. Primaries show dark tips, creating a dark wedge on outer wing in flight. Winter adults have a white forehead and mottled grey cap. Juveniles are similar to winter adults but with ginger mottling to upperparts and a paler orange black-tipped bill.

KEY FACT The very similar Arctic Tern has a shorter bill with no black on its tip, shorter red legs, and no dark patches on the primaries when seen in flight.

LOCATION	DATE/TIME

STATUS AND HABITS

Common Terns are elegant, slender-winged waterbirds with an easy, buoyant flight, and are summer visitors to Britain from overwintering sites in tropical West Africa. Nesting sites are usually shingle banks, sometimes away from water, and can be near coasts or well inland. The birds readily take to artificial floating platforms in reservoirs and gravel pits, and will travel considerable distances to fish. Colonial in habits, they will sometimes be found near Black-headed Gulls.

BLACK TERN
Chlidonias niger

FACT FILE

SIZE Length 22–24cm HABITAT Fresh or brackish marshes with rich vegetation FOOD Insect and aquatic invertebrates, tiny fish and amphibians VOICE Harsh, squeaky *kik-keek* calls; various short contact notes

IDENTIFICATION

A small tern with a short, scarcely forked tail. Summer adults are dark slaty grey with an almost black head and very dark upper wing, and a paler grey rump and tail. Long, slender bill is black but short legs are red. Winter plumage is much paler, with a white underside and black smudge near shoulder. Juveniles resemble winter adults but with darker shoulders and some brown in wings.

KEY FACT Both the White-winged Black Tern and Whiskered Tern may also turn up in Britain on migration. Although similar in size and habits to the Black Tern, they lack that species' overall dark plumage and are far less common.

LOCATION	DATE/TIME

STATUS AND HABITS

The Black Tern is most common on large lakes and marshes in E Europe, but colonies are found in the Netherlands, and returning summer migrants often overshoot and arrive in Britain. In autumn, juvenile birds may also stop over on marshes and estuaries. These small terns are adept at catching insects and larvae in or above fresh water, hovering with ease, but also having a very agile flight, this enabling them to hawk for emerging aquatic insects. Their winters are spent in tropical West Africa.

SWIFT
Apus apus

FACT FILE

SIZE Length 16–17cm HABITAT Almost entirely aerial, but nests in urban sites FOOD Flying insects, drifting airborne spiders VOICE High-pitched, shrill, screaming whistle in breeding season

IDENTIFICATION

Adult plumage is almost all dull brown, apart from a small white throat patch and greyish forehead. In flight, deeply forked tail shows clearly, and wings look long, narrow, crescent-shaped and swept back. Legs are very short and never seen in flight. Juveniles are almost identical to adults, but in good light upper feathers show pale margins.

LOCATION	DATE/TIME

KEY FACT

Swifts are the last migrants to arrive in Britain in springtime, and among the first to leave towards the end of Aug, when they head to sub-Saharan Africa for the winter.

STATUS AND HABITS

The Swift spends almost its entire life in the air, apart from when nest-building, incubating and caring for the nestlings. Food is captured on the wing, and birds can also sleep on the wing, climbing to great heights to do this. They sometimes swoop low over water to drink, and often gather in feeding flocks over lakes and rivers when aquatic insects like mayflies are emerging. Nestlings grow quickly on a diet of insects, and can enter periods of torpor when food supplies are low.

KINGFISHER
Alcedo atthis

FACT FILE

SIZE Length 16–17cm **HABITAT** Streams, rivers, lakes; sometimes coasts in winter **FOOD** Mostly small freshwater fish, some insect larvae **VOICE** Shrill, whistling flight call; quiet, bubbling song

KEY FACT When suitable perches are not available, Kingfishers can hover briefly over the water on rapid wingbeats to look for prey. They then fly off rapidly, giving their shrill, whistling call.

IDENTIFICATION
Adults have bright blue upperparts, including crown, nape and moustache. Back is slightly paler and shiny, and there are indistinct white spots on wings and crown. Face and most of underside are rich orange-chestnut, but with whitish patches on side of neck and under chin. Legs and feet are coral red. Sexes are alike, but long, dagger-like bill is all black in male and with a reddish base in female. Juveniles are duller than adults.

LOCATION	DATE/TIME

STATUS AND HABITS

The Kingfisher's large head and bill look out of proportion to the compact body, short tail and short red legs, but these are perfect adaptations to its way of life, enabling it to perch on twigs over water, dive for small fish or fly rapidly along streams. Submerging completely, Kingfishers can easily take small fish in quite shallow water; they take their prey to a perch, where it will be killed and swallowed. Nests are built in tunnels dug out of sandy river banks.

SAND MARTIN
Riparia riparia

FACT FILE

SIZE Length 12cm HABITAT Feeds aerially; nests in sandy banks near water FOOD Small flying insects, drifting spiders VOICE Various quiet sounds, including grating contact calls; harsh, twittering song

IDENTIFICATION

A small, compact bird with a short slightly forked tail and broad wings. Adults are dark greyish brown above with sandy tones in good light. Cheeks and breast-band are lighter brown, and rest of underside is white with slight blotching on flanks and brownish speckles on throat. In flight, underwing looks dusky brown. Legs, feet and bill are black. Juveniles are similar but with pale feather fringes.

KEY FACT Sand Martins are very widespread across Britain and Europe, with colonies forming wherever there are suitable nesting sites, and can be found in a wide range of habitats, including many man-made sites.

LOCATION	DATE/TIME

STATUS AND HABITS

Sand Martins are among the earliest migrants to arrive in Britain in spring and are regularly seen skimming low over the water on large lakes and reservoirs. Nesting colonially in sandy banks, they often return to the same site, but will also readily take to artificial sites such as drainpipes or specially made colonies. Nesting sites may be at some distance from water, but they seem to prefer feeding over water. In autumn, they gather in very large flocks before migrating back to sub-Saharan Africa.

SWALLOW
Hirundo rustica

FACT FILE

SIZE Length 17–19cm HABITAT Aerial, over farmland, water, villages FOOD Flying insects VOICE Short *chit* alarm notes; quiet warbling song

KEY FACT Swallows leave Britain in the autumn, sometimes gathering in excited, chattering flocks on wires, before heading **S** on a long journey to the **S** half of Africa. They arrive there in time for the most abundant supply of insects.

IDENTIFICATION
From below, shows a long, forked tail with long streamers, narrow wings and a short beak. Underside is mostly buff-white with a dark, shiny blue-black breast-band, and a rich red throat, chin and forehead. Upperparts are shiny blue-black, and spread tail shows white spots on inner feathers. Sexes are alike but female has shorter tail streamers. Juveniles are similar to adults but colours are less intense and tail is shorter.

LOCATION	DATE/TIME

STATUS AND HABITS

A very widespread bird, the
Swallow arrives in Britain in
spring and disperses into a
wide range of habitats, although
it is most often seen hawking
for insects over pastures and
water, especially when there is
a hatch of aquatic insects. Food
is sometimes caught very low
over the water, particularly
in poor weather. Nests are
constructed in open buildings,
under eaves or on ledges, and
birds are often seen perching
on wires nearby. Mud pellets
are collected from puddles or
river banks for nest-building.

WATER PIPIT
Anthus spinoletta

SIZE Length 17–18cm HABITAT Winter visitor on lowland wetlands FOOD Mainly insects, but some seeds and plant material VOICE Harsh *tseep* calls; pleasant, melodious song

FACT FILE

IDENTIFICATION
Spring adults have greyish-brown upperparts and a double white wingbar formed by pale edges to coverts. Tail is dark with white outer edges. Underside is mostly dull white but with a pinkish tinge to breast. Legs and bill are dark brown. Winter adults look browner above and lack pink on underside, showing more streaks on breast. Juveniles are similar to winter adults but with clearer markings.

WINTER

LOCATION	DATE/TIME

STATUS AND HABITS

Once thought to be the same species as the Rock Pipit, the Water Pipit is now recognised as a distinct species. Breeding in the high mountains of Spain, the Alps and ranges further E, birds migrate down to lower altitudes in winter, but are almost always found near water. Some individuals migrate over longer distances and end up in S Britain, where they favour wet meadows, tidal creeks and ice-free streams; they may also feed on coasts alongside Rock Pipits.

KEY FACT

A favourite habitat for Water Pipits overwintering in Britain is a Watercress bed, where the constantly running water is always free of ice and the abundance of invertebrates provides plenty of food.

SUMMER

MEADOW PIPIT
Anthus pratensis

SIZE Length 14.5cm **HABITAT** Open grasslands, bogs, marshes **FOOD** Mostly invertebrates; some seeds in winter **VOICE** Quiet *tsip* calls; whistling flight calls

FACT FILE

IDENTIFICATION

Adults have mostly olive-brown upperparts, grading into darker buff-brown with darker streaks on crown and back. Rump is brighter olive-brown. Underparts are greyish white with olive tinges, and a chest-band of dark spots and streaks extending onto flanks. Legs are pinkish buff and bill is grey-brown. Juveniles have heavier streaking on upperparts and clearer pale margins on wing feathers.

LOCATION	DATE/TIME

STATUS AND HABITS

Meadow Pipits are widespread and common in suitable habitats, but are easily overlooked owing to their coloration, which helps them blend perfectly with grassland vegetation. If alarmed, they fly off quickly and dive into cover, giving their characteristic *tsip* calls. Neatly constructed grassy nests lined with hair are hidden in dense vegetation, the only clue to breeding birds being the spring song and display flight. In winter, they may mix with other pipits to feed on strand-lines, on the edge of lakes and on marshes.

KEY FACT The Meadow Pipit sings in flight, starting from a high point and 'parachuting' down while delivering its short, melodious song, which ends in a descending scale.

PIED WAGTAIL
Motacilla alba yarellii

FACT FILE

SIZE Length 18cm HABITAT Mainly near water; some urban sites FOOD Small invertebrates VOICE Loud *chizzick* contact notes; rapid warbling, twittering song

IDENTIFICATION

Breeding male has black on crown, nape, chin and upper breast. Upperparts are mostly black but with white fringes to wing feathers and outer-tail feathers. Breeding female is similar but with a greyer back. Non-breeding adults lack black throat. Juveniles are similar to non-breeding female but with a browner tinge to plumage and buff fringes on larger wing feathers.

WINTER MALE

LOCATION	DATE/TIME

KEY FACT

At night Pied Wagtails often gather in large flocks for communal roosting, favouring sheltered reedbeds, sewage plants or even town centre buildings where there may be some warmth.

STATUS AND HABITS

This is the British and Irish subspecies of the White Wagtail, a very widespread bird across Continental Europe. Active and lively, Pied Wagtails are easily spotted as they feed on insects, sometimes making short dashes along the ground to catch them. Their swooping flight and frequent calls also draw attention. They prefer to feed in open habitats where insects are plentiful, and can be found in city parks and urban sites as well as beside water. Nests are built in natural or artificial crevices.

SUMMER

GREY WAGTAIL
Motacilla cinerea

FACT FILE

SIZE Length 18–19cm **HABITAT** Running water, mill races, stony lake margins **FOOD** Mainly insects and spiders, some aquatic invertebrates **VOICE** Shrill *cheee* contact notes; thin, high-pitched song

IDENTIFICATION

Adult male is mostly grey above with an olive-yellow rump, black bib and white stripes above and below eye. Underside is mostly lemon yellow with greyish flanks. Female and non-breeding male have a paler bib or white throat, and buff tones to underside. All plumages have flesh-coloured legs and feet, and a dark bill. Juveniles are similar to non-breeding adults but with buff fringes to wing feathers.

SUMMER MALE

LOCATION	DATE/TIME

KEY FACT

Grey Wagtails are resident through much of Britain and Ireland, but birds in the N of the region may migrate S in the winter, when more individuals may be seen on the coast.

STATUS AND HABITS

Grey Wagtails are frequently seen beside rushing water, sometimes standing on mossy rocks, their tails and rear ends bobbing up and down repeatedly. They dash out over the water with a swooping flight to catch emerging insects, before returning to a favourite perch. In flight, the upper wing shows a white wingbar and the long black tail has broad white margins. Nests are usually built in crevices close to water, often in man-made structures such as bridges, and are found in urban sites as well as wilder upland regions.

WINTER MALE

YELLOW WAGTAIL
Motacilla flava

FACT FILE

SIZE Length 17cm HABITAT Lowland wetlands, watermeadows, damp grasslands, dune slacks FOOD Small invertebrates VOICE Shrill *pseep* calls; short, twittering song

IDENTIFICATION

Smallest and most compact wagtail, with a neat, pipit-like silhouette. Adult male is conspicuously bright yellow below, but with a greenish-yellow cap and mantle, greyish-green wings and a darker tail with lighter outer feathers. Bill and legs are dark. Female and juveniles are duller yellow than males, with more olive tones, and base of bill is paler in juveniles.

KEY FACT Male Yellow Wagtails show distinctive head patterns and colours across the species' European range, varying from blue-grey to black; birds of these races occasionally arrive in Britain in spring.

MALE

LOCATION	DATE/TIME

STATUS AND HABITS

The Yellow Wagtail is a widespread but declining summer visitor to lowland areas of England, becoming more scarce further N and W. It prefers large wet meadows with grazing animals present, and in spring males can often be seen on fenceposts giving their display song. Grassy nests are built on the ground in small hollows. Birds can be seen searching for insects among animal dung and also making short flights in pursuit of prey. In autumn, they gather on coastal strand-lines to feed before heading S to Africa.

FEMALE

DIPPER
Cinclus cinclus

SIZE Length 18cm **HABITAT** Fast-flowing rocky rivers and streams, mostly in uplands **FOOD** Mainly aquatic invertebrates, but also fish fry and worms **VOICE** Sharp *tzit* calls and pleasant warbling song

FACT FILE

IDENTIFICATION

Has a compact, plump silhouette with short, rounded wings and a cocked tail. Adults appear all dark above and white below, but head and neck are dark brown, and back, wings and tail are dark slate grey with black feather margins. White eyelid shows when blinking. Chin, throat and breast are pure white, but belly is brown, becoming darker under tail. Juveniles have a greyer mottled appearance.

LOCATION	DATE/TIME

STATUS AND HABITS

Dippers are almost always found along fast-flowing streams and rivers, living up to their name with their constant tail-bobbing, and also by dipping under the water to feed. They are able to swim, and also walk along the riverbed against the current, foraging for food among stones.

Nests are usually built under bridges or in crevices on the bank. Stones with white droppings on them indicate individuals' favourite perches in the river. Most birds are resident, moving to lowland valleys in winter.

JUVENILE

CETTI'S WARBLER
Cettia cetti

FACT FILE

SIZE Length 13.5cm **HABITAT** Bushy areas close to water and reedbeds **FOOD** Mainly insects, but also some spiders and worms **VOICE** Explosive, loud burst of song; sharp *chip* calls

IDENTIFICATION

A large warbler with uniform chestnut-brown upperparts and wings. Has an off-white supercilium, and whitish underparts grading into grey-brown on flanks and under tail. Undertail coverts have dull white tips, which show when tail is cocked. Bill is dark brown and legs dark brownish buff. Sexes are similar but males are heavier than females.

LOCATION	DATE/TIME

KEY FACT

Once a scarce visitor to Britain, Cetti's Warblers are now resident – unlike many warblers, they do not migrate. They can be found in freshwater marshes over a wide area of S England, with occasional sightings further N.

STATUS AND HABITS

The explosive burst of song, considered to be the loudest of any small bird, is the best way to locate the otherwise secretive Cetti's Warbler, which spends most of its time in dense cover near water or reedbeds. Males may mate with more than one female and take no part in rearing the young. Nests are built in dense vegetation and, unusually for warblers, the females lay red eggs. Singing males may occasionally be glimpsed in gaps in vegetation, but otherwise they remain hidden and difficult to see.

GRASSHOPPER WARBLER
Locustella naevia

FACT FILE

SIZE Length 12.5cm HABITAT Undergrowth in wet meadows, hedgerows and ditches, boggy plantations FOOD Mostly insects, but some spiders, centipedes and small worms VOICE Very high-pitched, reeling, trilling song; short *pitt* calls

IDENTIFICATION

A small, fairly uniformly coloured warbler with olive-brown upperparts streaked with darker brown blotches. Wings are darker brown, with buff or reddish fringes to feathers, and tail is reddish brown with indistinct dark bars. Chin and throat are much paler. Blackish-brown bill has a yellow base, and legs are pale yellowish brown.

LOCATION	DATE/TIME

STATUS AND HABITS

Its brownish colours and secretive habits make this a very difficult bird to detect in marshy grasslands, but the distinctive call (inaudible to some) is the best clue to its location. Resembling the sound of a winding fisherman's reel or a grasshopper's song, the call is a rapid series of high notes (as many as 26 per second) reeled off for minutes on end, and carrying for up to 1km in still conditions. The bird turns its head from side to side, making it difficult to pinpoint.

KEY FACT

Grasshopper Warblers arrive from Africa in mid-Apr, and the male's song can be heard night and day (but mostly at dusk and dawn) until Jul. Singing birds can sometimes be approached quite closely.

SEDGE WARBLER
Acrocephalus schoenobaenus

FACT FILE

SIZE Length 13cm HABITAT Reedbeds, thick waterside vegetation FOOD Insects, spiders VOICE Harsh *tuc* and *churr* alarm calls; rapid song of mixed harsh and musical notes

IDENTIFICATION
Adults have strongly marked upperparts, with an olive-brown nape and dark-streaked mantle and scapulars, but rump is tawny brown and unmarked. Head has a black-streaked crown and long white supercilium. Underside is off-white, paler on throat and belly. Legs are greyish and bill is black with a paler base. Juveniles resemble adults but with yellower underparts and brown spots on breast.

KEY FACT
Sedge Warblers are territorial in winter and summer, defending their feeding and breeding areas, with males singing loudly from prominent perches and keeping a lookout for intruders.

LOCATION	DATE/TIME

STATUS AND HABITS

A very common and widespread warbler, found in a range of wetland habitats from large reedbeds to ditches and small ponds. Birds arrive in spring from overwintering sites in Africa and take up territory; males often sing from open perches and can sometimes be approached quite closely. Nests are built low in dense waterside vegetation and both birds help care for the young. Breeding success varies each year depending on insect abundance, but overwintering birds may suffer from drought conditions in Africa.

REED WARBLER
Acrocephalus scirpaceus

FACT FILE

SIZE Length 13cm HABITAT Reedbeds, dense waterside sedges FOOD Insects, spiders, tiny snails VOICE Low, guttural, churring song with varied phrases; harsh alarm calls

IDENTIFICATION

Adults of this medium-sized warbler have uniform olive-brown upperparts and a rufous-tinged rump, and darker tones to primary wing feathers. Underside is white, with buff tones on flanks and undertail. Legs are greyish brown, and bill is dark with a paler base. Feathers on head can be fluffed up when singing to give a 'peaked' effect. Juveniles look brighter than adults, but with a less distinct face pattern.

LOCATION	DATE/TIME

STATUS AND HABITS

Reed Warblers can easily be heard singing in reedbeds in spring and early summer, but are more difficult to spot as they cling to vertical reed stems and move around in dense vegetation in search of insects. Nests are deep cups of grass and reed flowers, neatly woven around several reed stems and hidden deep in the reedbeds. Found mainly in S England and Wales, these birds are starting to spread to other habitats, such as waterside stands of willowherb and crops of Oilseed Rape.

KEY FACT

The Reed Warbler's legs are sturdy and their feet have a very wide spread, enabling them to cling to vertical reed stems and move up and down quickly or hop from one plant to another.

MARSH WARBLER
Acrocephalus palustris

SIZE Length 13cm HABITAT Dense, low waterside vegetation, Common Nettle patches, Osiers FOOD Small insects and spiders, some snails, berries VOICE Prolonged musical song with some mimicry; *tchuc* alarm notes

FACT FILE

IDENTIFICATION

A medium-sized warbler, very similar to Reed Warbler and difficult to separate unless seen closely. Has more olive tones in upperparts than Reed Warbler and no rufous tones in rump. Bill is slightly shorter with a wider base, and head looks more rounded. In profile, looks fuller-bodied than Reed Warbler and is slightly heavier.

LOCATION	DATE/TIME

KEY FACT An average Marsh Warbler song repertoire may consist of mimicry of more than 70 other bird songs, of which at least 40 will be African species and 30 will be European species.

STATUS AND HABITS

The Marsh Warbler is a scarce summer visitor to Britain, found in only a few scattered localities in the S, arriving late in spring and leaving before many other migrants in Aug. Males announce their arrival with long bouts of singing; the song is a distinctive, lively torrent of chattering and musical notes, with much mimicry of other birds, including species heard on overwintering grounds in Africa. Nests are built in dense vegetation and are untidy cups of grasses, fixed to stems by woven 'handles'.

BEARDED TIT
Panurus biarmicus

FACT FILE

SIZE Length 14–15.5cm HABITAT Extensive reedbeds FOOD Invertebrates in summer; seeds in autumn and winter VOICE Quiet song, difficult to detect; explosive *ping* calls, often heard

MALE

IDENTIFICATION
Short-winged and long-tailed with mostly tawny-russet plumage. Adult male has a grey head and bold black 'moustache' of loose feathers contrasting with white chin and throat. Tail is graduated, with white feather tips. Wings look banded owing to black and white patterns on flight feathers and tertials. Female lacks male's head pattern and has duller tones. Juveniles resemble female and have black and white wing coverts.

KEY FACT The rounded wings have a distinct pattern in flight, with a rufous central panel bordered with white on the 'shoulders' and with black on the tertials. The long, tapering tail has white margins.

LOCATION	DATE/TIME

STATUS AND HABITS

Bearded Tits (sometimes known as Bearded Reedlings) are totally dependent on large reedbeds and are very susceptible to harsh winter weather, so they occur mainly in isolated populations in S parts of Britain. Nesting together in loose colonies, they are often spotted in small foraging flocks or flying low over the reeds on whirring wingbeats, making the metallic calls that have led birders to nickname them 'pingers'. Outside the breeding season they may form quite large flocks.

MALE

REED BUNTING
Emberiza schoeniclus

FACT FILE

SIZE Length 15–16cm **HABITAT** River banks, ditches, lake and pond margins **FOOD** Small invertebrates and seeds **VOICE** Thin *tseep* calls; short metallic-sounding song

IDENTIFICATION

Breeding male is distinctive, with a black bill, black head, white collar and white 'moustache'. Back is brown with darker streaks and a grey rump. Underside is mostly white with some spotting on flanks. Winter male has a browner head. Female has a brown head with darker stripes and black and white moustachial stripes, and similar upperparts to male. Juveniles resemble female but with less distinct head markings.

MALE

STATUS AND HABITS

Reed Buntings are resident in Britain, but birds from further N and E in Continental Europe and Scandinavia may arrive in winter, when they gather in large flocks, sometimes with other species of sparrows and buntings, and can easily be overlooked. Territorial in the breeding season, the birds build nests low in dense vegetation, not always near water, but often alongside streams or reedbeds. They are less likely to be associated with water in winter, when they sometimes move to stubble fields to feed, or visit garden bird tables.

LOCATION	DATE/TIME

KEY FACT

The Reed Bunting earned its alternative common name of Parson of the Marshes from its distinctive white collar, seen easily when males sit on prominent perches in open marshland to sing their repetitive song in spring.

MALE

Common names are in plain text and scientific names are in *italic*.

PHOTOGRAPHIC ACKNOWLEDGEMENTS

Photographs supplied by Nature Photographers Ltd. All photographs by Paul Sterry except for the those on the following pages:

Colin Carver: 187; Andrew Cleave: 75; Andrew Merrick: 151; Owen Newman: 90; David Osborn: 86, 87; Richard Revels: 71; James Sutherland: 142; Roger Tidman: 27, 81, 88 (left), 99, 156 (right), 160, 168, 186; Derek Washington: 153.